# INTRODUCTION TO BUSINESS CONSULTING

# INTRODUCTION TO BUSINESS CONSULTING

FIRST EDITION

Carl Garrison, Joseph Ivison, James Rather, and Carl Scott

**cognella®**

SAN DIEGO

Bassim Hamadeh, CEO and Publisher
John Remington, Senior Acquisitions Editor
Gem Rabanera, Senior Project Editor / Associate Editor
Jeanine Rees, Production Editor
Jess Estrella, Senior Graphic Designer
JoHannah McDonald, Licensing Coordinator
Natalie Piccotti, Director of Marketing
Kassie Graves, Senior Vice President, Editorial
Jamie Giganti, Director of Academic Publishing

cognella® | ACADEMIC PUBLISHING
320 South Cedros Ave., Ste. 400, Solana Beach, CA 92075

# Brief Contents

# Detailed Contents

## CHAPTER 1

# Introduction

## Why Business Consulting?

The business consulting industry is a huge industry. Worldwide, the industry accounts for some $449 billion (Open Business Council, 2022). In the United States alone, industry accounts for some $303 billion when you include management, scientific, technical, and accounting/tax preparation.

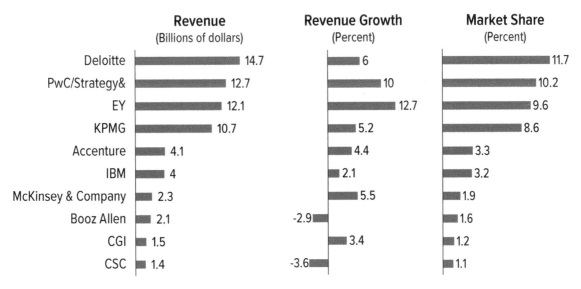

FIGURE 1.1  Top consulting firms by revenue

The need for consultants familiar with how to consult has never been greater. There are many attractive features to business consulting, including the following:

- It is a chance to be on your own, with minimum involvement in organizational politics, red tape, and bosses

- It requires little capital

- It can allow you to control your time; the number of hours and days you work; the time of day or night you work

- It presents the opportunity for variety and travel

- It does not have a mandatory or traditional retirement age

- It can provide a very handsome annual income.

Because it is so attractive, competition is very intense. Before you decide to become a consultant, this book and attending a course on the subject will aid in determining whether to follow the sweet siren song of consulting.

We have all heard about consultants and consulting, but few of us clearly know what is involved. What we need is an overview of the field. Certain characteristics are common to all or most consultants. But before we do, we should set the scene. A client has hired the services of a consultant to achieve a particular goal, which is called an intervention. A client can be an organization or an individual; an intervention may be a report, a teaching program, a change in organization procedure or structure, or a selection of hardware or software, etc. The person who brings about the intervention is the consultant, who possesses certain qualities. These qualities include the follwing:

- Expertise in a particular area in which the client is lacking

- An outsider—outside the structure of the client organization

- An adviser—consultants do not have the authority to bring change directly; they act by getting the client to accept their recommendations

Consultants are used in every field, however small or large. Below is a partial list of some of the kinds of organizations that hire consultants.

- Nonprofit organizations

- Large corporations or government organizations

- Divisions of large corporations

- Schools and colleges

- Health care institutions

- Entertainment industries

- Advertising agencies

- Small-business firms

Below is a list of some of the reasons a client might hire a consultant.

- Identify problems

- Propose solutions

- Bring specific knowledge

- Suggest changes

- Instruct staff on changes

- Teach new technologies to the workforce

It is evident that to satisfy the needs of a client, a consultant must possess specific skills. They include the follwing:

- Technical skills

- Interpersonal skills

- Marketing skills

- Consulting skills; determine client needs, identify problems and solutions, gather data, define the problem, diagnose the problem, and present data to the client

This text aims to help people become consultants by introducing them to the key ideas of consulting.

## Using This Text

The authors created this text to be used for instruction as well as a resource for consultants. Each chapter covers a different aspect of business consulting. The consultant may follow the text or selected chapters for review and use as a reference. The topics covered in the text are:

**Consultants' career options.** There are three primary career paths for a consultant, and each path is discussed in detail in Chapter 2.

**Communicate with the client.** The text introduces each person's communication style, how to recognize them, and how to use the knowledge to persuade them to your ideas and lead to better communication with the client. This is discussed in Chapter 3.

**Determine client needs.** The key to a consulting assignment is understanding the client's needs. Chapter 4 will introduce a structured approach to uncovering and developing client needs.

**Manage stakeholder expectations.** Understanding and managing the stakeholders is key to the success of the consultant engagement. Chapter 5 helps you identify stakeholders and understand their needs for a successful project.

**Define the problem and develop a letter of agreement.** Chapter 4 introduces the approach to understanding the client's needs. Chapter 6 guides the reader in defining the client's problem associated with the need. Chapter 7 gives an example of putting the need and problem resolution into a contract called a Letter of Understanding with the client.

**Manage a consulting project.** Chapter 8 discusses ways to manage a consulting project and information about the various methodologies involved.

**Develop hypotheses.** The "secret sauce" of business consulting is determining various hypotheses to solve the client's issues. This is detailed in Chapter 9.

**Test the hypotheses.** Once hypotheses have been defined, they must be proved or disproved. A structured approach for testing the hypotheses is discussed in Chapter 10.

**Presenting a consulting report to the client.** Defining what should be in a consultant report and the presentation to a client is detailed in Chapter 11.

**Starting a business.** The information needed to create a consulting business is presented in Chapter 12.

**Going to the next level.** The ideas, attitudes, and skills to become a "Trusted Adviser"—the desired end-state of the consultant's relationship with a client—are presented in Chapter 13.

**Resources for a consultant.** Chapter 14 contains tools, techniques, and processes for conducting a consulting engagement successfully. In addition, it includes a detailed case study that can be used to apply and test the knowledge learned in other parts of the text.

## BIBLIOGRAPHY

Baca, Claudia. *Project Manager's Spotlight on Change Management*. San Francisco: Harbour Light Press, 2005.

Biech, Elaine. *The Business of Consulting, The Basics and Beyond*. San Francisco: John Wiley & Sons, 2007.

Block, Peter. *Flawless Consulting: A Guide to Getting Your Expertise Used*. San Diego: University Associates, 1981.

———. *The Flawless Consulting Fieldbook and Companion: A Guide to Understanding Your Expertise*. San Francisco: Jossey-Bass/Pfeiffer, 2001.

Cheng, Victor. *Case Interview Secrets: A Former McKinsey Interviewer Reveals How to Get Multiple Job Offers in Consulting*. Seattle: Innovation Press, 2012.

Friga, Paul N. *The McKinsey Engagement: A Powerful Toolkit for More Efficient and Effective Team Problem Solving*. New York: McGraw-Hill, 2009.

Maister, David H. *The Trusted Advisor*. New York: Simon & Schuster, 2000.

Open Business Council. *Overview of the Global Consulting Industry Market*. June 1, 2022. Accessed June 2, 2022. https://www.openbusinesscouncil.org/consulting-industry-market-research/.

Rasiel, Ethan M. *The McKinsey Way: Using the Techniques of the World's Top Strategic Consultants*. New York: McGraw-Hill, 1999.

Statista Research Department. *Consulting Services Industry in the U.S.—Statistics & Facts*. February 22, 2022. Accessed May 3, 2022. https://www.statista.com/topics/2247/consulting-services-industry-in-the-us/.

Stroh, Linda K., and Homer H. Johnson. *The Basic Principles of Effective Consulting*. New York: Psychology Press, 2015.

Weinberg, Gerald M. *The Secrets of Consulting*. New York: Dorset House, 1985.

# Consultant Careers

## Introduction

The dictionary defines a consultant as "an expert in a particular field who works as an advisor either to a company or another individual." It sounds pretty vague, doesn't it? Let's explore the job duties of a consultant. The job duties of a business consultant include forming solutions or recommendations to solve problems and presenting those analyses to the business/organization. A consultant works closely with the business/organization owner/director and employees to gather information to assess what changes are needed to solve problems, improve the business, and reach goals. What are the skills required for consulting?

Desired skills and attributes a consultant needs are the following:

- You must be a people person—a large part of this job involves being on the phone and meeting with startup entrepreneurs to executive management in large companies/organizations. Obviously, consultants engage in a fair amount of email communication.

- You can provide solutions to problems and resolve issues diplomatically at the highest level.

- You possess vital research and strategic analysis skills.

- You can analyze data, determine trends and applications, and report them clearly and correctly.

- You are capable of working in a fast-paced environment.

- You possess strong interpersonal skills and the ability to develop working relationships quickly.

- You embrace teamwork (clients and self) and thrive in a self-motivated environment.

- You have an innate desire to continually improve and add value—not only as a person but also through the projects you're working on.

- You have marketing skills and attitudes that you can sell yourself and services to others with a need.

Some people are confused about what a consultant is as opposed to a contractor. The difference is that a consultant's role is to evaluate a client's needs and provide expert advice and opinion on what needs to be done. The **contractor's** role is to assess the client's needs and perform the work. A **consultant** develops findings, conclusions, and recommendations for client consideration and decision-making as an advisory service.

There are three primary consultant career paths:

- Entrepreneur

- Corporate

- Internal

An **entrepreneur consultant** is external to the organization contracting for advisory services. They practice their trade either alone or in a small partnership. The consultant's relationship with the organization is usually determined by a project's contract or Letter of Agreement. Consultants are paid based on a particular project having specific desired results and deliverables from the consultant. Payroll taxes are not withheld from the person's paycheck; the person pays their own payroll taxes. They are an independent small business providing advisory services to all sizes of organizations. They must have consulting and business skills (accounting, marketing, management) to run a business.

A **corporate consultant** is also external to the organization contracting for advisory services. A **corporate consultant** is a consultant for a corporate firm in a business comprised of many industry-specific experts who offer professional advice, guidance, and actionable solutions to businesses experiencing issues they cannot deal with in-house. Example firms include the following:

- McKinsey & Company

- The Boston Consulting Group

- Bain & Company

- Booz & Company

- Deloitte Consulting

- PricewaterhouseCoopers

- Monitor Group

- Ernst & Young

- Mercer LLC

- Accenture

The corporate firm provides its consultants with marketing, accounting, billing, and research assistance. In addition, the corporate consultant provides direct advisory services for the client.

An **internal consultant** is considered an adviser (consultant) while being an ongoing member of the organization. The internal consultant is someone who operates within an organization but is available to consult in their areas of specialization by other departments or individuals (acting as clients). The internal consultant's relationship with the organization is usually determined by job descriptions and personnel policies. They are paid based on their ongoing role in the organization. Payroll taxes are withheld from the person's paychecks.

# Entrepreneur

## Entrepreneur Consultant

Entrepreneur consultants operate an independent practice as a one-person company or small partnership. To be an independent business, do you have the right stuff.

- Are you a self-starter? You do things on your own without someone prodding you.

- Do you like people? You get along with almost everyone.

- Can you lead or influence others? You can get most people to go along when you start something.

- Can you take responsibility? You like to take charge and see them through.

- Are you a good organizer? You like to have a plan before you start. So you are usually the one to get things lined up when the group wants to do something.

- Are you a hard worker? You can keep going as long as it takes to accomplish a task.

- Can you make decisions? You can make up your mind in a hurry if you need to.

- Can people trust what you say? You don't say things you don't mean and are not valid.

- Can you stick with it? You can make up your mind to do something, and nothing will stop you.

- Do you have good health? You have good health and lots of energy.

There are many attractive features to being an entrepreneur consultant, just as there are some unattractive ones. But first, let us look at the positive side of consulting.

- It is a chance to be on your own, with minimum involvement in organization politics, red tape, and bosses.

- It requires little capital investment.

- It can allow you to control your time: the number of hours and days you work; the time of day or night you work.

- It presents the opportunity for variety and travel.

- It does not have a mandatory or traditional retirement age.

- It can provide a handsome annual income: some successful consultants earn $150,000 a year for what some describe as "part-time work."

Consulting and running a business may not be for everybody. Now let's look at some of the negatives involved.

- Because it is so attractive, competition is very intense.

- Because you are on your own, you do not have the support system of an organization.

- Because you are outside the power structures of an organization, you lack the authority to impose solutions on others—everything is about influencing others.

- Because you can control your time, you do not have a regimen or schedule imposed on you from the outside that you must conform to (some of the time, clients set a schedule).

- Because your time is your own, you may find that the distinction between working time and leisure time is lost; your time may be your client's time.

- Because when you are working on a project (billable time), you are not marketing, and when you are marketing, you are not billable. It can be hard to balance.

**Entrepreneur consultants** are self-employed or part of a team (partnership).

Many consultants are self-employed (entrepreneur) or associated with other consultants in a consulting team (partnership). A group of consultants can supplement the skills and expertise of each of its members and thereby provide a client with both a wide range and an in-depth knowledge of the areas of concern. But, of course, there are times when the scope and depth are not required, and then the single consultant works best for the client.

In either case, consultants are hired by the client for a specific purpose and generally for a limited time. Whether as individuals or parts of a team, consultants have to take special care to be sensitive to their clients' attitudes, the possibility of resentment toward staff members, and the informal power structures within client organizations.

Because consultants are outsiders, they may be seen as intruders and may encounter mistrust, negative feelings, resentment, irritability, or uncooperative behavior. Moreover, consultants are usually engaged by clients for too short a period to become intimately familiar with the local style of client organizations.

Consultants, therefore, must use care in the way they relate to members of their client organizations. Consultants do not have the authority to bring about change directly or implement programs. Instead, they must act through others by obtaining the client's consent to recommendations. This means they must persuade the client of their interpretation of a problem and the value of their suggested solution. It is this lack of direct power that, in part, distinguishes consultants from managers. Instead of being directly involved in carrying out a task or program, as managers are, consultants analyze situations, pinpoint problems, and propose solutions. In essence, consultants try to use influence without authority to gain the desired objective.

## Forms of a Consulting Business

There are two basic approaches to entrepreneur consulting:

- A one-person firm
- A partnership of a few consultants

## The One-Person Firm

It often seems that being a one-person show will give you the ultimate freedom.

- You have no boss—except your clients.
- You can allocate your time however you wish—except when a client is pressing you for results.
- You can have a variety of jobs—except when you get typecast.
- You have no organizational worries—except to understand your client's organization.
- You can do only the type of work you love—except for the nitty-gritty of running a small business.
- You have no overhead costs—except the ongoing cost of your unbilled time (while you are making contacts, doing mailings, running ads, doing your bookkeeping, or just waiting for business).

The one-person shop probably works best if you aim at a relatively narrow, technical field where your expertise is prominent or well known, and a team effort is unnecessary. However, there are drawbacks to being a loner. One of them is getting lonesome, emotionally and intellectually. Very successful loners often give up all their freedom and join a team (partnership or firm) to enjoy the simulation of collegial relationships. Another is landing work too broad in scope or too big and urgent to handle alone. And, of course, the one-person company has a ceiling of growth.

A limited liability corporation (LLC) is the purest form of legal arrangement for the one-person consulting practice and to shelter your liabilities. Many operate as sole proprietors. The primary difference is the liability.

## Partnership

Sometimes, a one-person operation is not the best way to go, perhaps because, as a personality, you need other people around you, or perhaps for different reasons. In that case, you might want to consider a partnership. Here are some of the benefits and drawbacks of a partnership.

- A partner can bring in business and share some of their contacts with you. But they will expect the same in return and may someday become a competitor.
- A partner will share responsibilities with you, but their actions are legally binding on you, and you may not be happy with them.

- A partner will broaden your scope, making you valuable to a broader range of clients. But your partner may also require your aid in situations where you are uncomfortable.

- A partner can help in a crisis, but you, in turn, have to help them in an emergency, and this demand may come at the worst time for you.

- A partner can provide you with much-needed friendship and peer support. But they might also come into conflict with you over personal matters and thus poison your working relationship.

## Corporate Consulting

A **corporate consultant** is also external to the organization contracting for advisory services. A corporate consultant is an employee of a corporate consulting firm. The relationship of the corporate consultant to the client organization is usually determined by a project's contract or Letter of Agreement. They are paid based on a particular project having specific desired results and deliverables from the corporate consulting firm. Corporate consultants are generally involved in work areas such as marketing, human resources, management, finance, information technology, and accounting. In addition, corporate consultants are responsible for improving companies' operations by assessing weaknesses and recommending business solutions.

Compared to other jobs, corporate consultant careers are projected to have a growth rate described as "much faster than average" at 14% from 2018 through 2028, according to the Bureau of Labor Statistics. As a result, the projected number of opportunities for a corporate consultant by 2028 is 118,300.

The most common skills found on corporate consultant résumés are:

- Project Management; 12%

- Financial Statements and Analysis; 10%

- Business Requirement Gathering; 8%

- Technology skills: Internet, PowerPoint, etc.; 16%

- Other particular knowledge or domain expertise; 54%

One of the significant advantages of being a corporate consultant versus an entrepreneur consultant is that other specialists in the firm handle marketing, research, and other issues. Also, corporate consultant firms provide regular payroll and benefits, such as health insurance, education funding, and paid vacations.

## Internal Consulting

**Internal consultants** are considered members of the organization. Their primary job is to assist other people working in other areas of the organization. Often these internal consultants are in large organizations and are from training and development, industrial engineering groups, or human resource departments. Internal consultants have several advantages over external firms, including a companywide perspective, continuity in implementation, the attraction of top talent to the company, higher levels of confidentiality, and greater cost-effectiveness. However, the typical small business usually does not have an extensive range of resources that warrant an internal consultant.

Like any corporate firm in need of business development, internal consultants need to build relationships with executives across the company and pitch proposals. Numerous funding models exist for internal consulting. Often internal consultant groups charge their total cost back to their "clients (other departments)." Before starting any engagement, clients should approve a statement of work and commit to paying the "fees" for the internal consulting team out of their budgets. The internal consultant should scope, staff, and deliver discrete projects with set start and completion dates and clear deliverables. Sticking to this principle is more complicated than it sounds. Avoid scope creep.

Consistently convincing internal clients that the advice provided is on par with, or exceeds, what they can get externally requires a culture of overachievement. You must foster this culture by defining explicit values, encouraging team members always to speak their minds and challenge each other, investing in a full training curriculum, seeking client feedback, and celebrating success.

To attract top talent, the internal consulting group will need a value proposition, such as unparalleled top-management exposure, tangible impact on strategy, a focus on professional development, the opportunity to transition into a management role in the technology industry after a minimum of two years with the group, and a fun team.

The differences between internal and external consultants are summarized in Table 2.1.

TABLE 2.1 **Consultant Type Comparison**

| Aspects | Internal Consultants | External Consultants |
| --- | --- | --- |
| Focus of attention | On desired outcomes from the project, maintaining one's job, and long-term relationships with other members | On desired results from the project, on retaining current and all clients, and short-term relationships with members |
| Client's perception of consultant skills | As another member with known roles, skills, and performance | As a specialist having strong expertise |
| Source of credibility with client | From the consultant's authority, known performance, and quality of relationships | From the consultant's reputation and apparent expertise |
| Biases of consultant | Influenced by the culture of the organization and the desires and personalities of other members | Influenced by personal and professional background |
| Consultant's knowledge base | Already knows much about the organization, in addition to having a specific professional knowledge | In addition to specific professional knowledge, one has to learn about the organization "from scratch" |
| Client's perception of consultant | As a member of the organization who also might be part of the problem | As an outsider, a "hired gun" who is not part of the problem |
| Client's acceptance of consultant | It depends on the top leadership's support of the project, consultant's authority, and the client's relationship with the consultant | It depends on the top leadership's support of the project and the skills of the consultant to get buy-in from members |

*(Continued)*

**TABLE 2.1** ( *Continued* )

| Aspects | Internal Consultants | External Consultants |
|---|---|---|
| Influence of consultant | It depends on the consultant's authority and expertise, and the client's relationship with the consultant | It depends on the top leadership's approval of the project and the consultant's interpersonal skills; the consultant has to learn about power and politics in the organization |
| Range of influence | Can often readily involve various resources throughout the organization | Operates within the scope and terms of the contract with the client |
| Options outside the project | Cannot readily opt out of the project | Can leave the project per any terms of the contract |

## The Marketing Challenge

Even in a big firm, the central problem of consulting is that you have to sell yourself. (That word *sell* is considered vulgar in many professional firms, and so they prefer stuffy euphemisms like "practice development." Marketing is a compromise term accepted in all but the stuffiest firms.)

In a non-consulting corporate career, maybe you will never have to sell. Fortunately, the "peddlers" (salesmen) handle that sort of "dirty work."

In consulting, however, it's up to you! Moreover, what you sell is mainly yourself—as a helpful person with some expertise. If you find the prospect of spending 20–50% of your time marketing a bit scary, unpleasant, or even humiliating, you should pursue a corporate firm for consulting where marketing is handled by specialists in that field; or seriously question your choice of consulting as a second career.

Even for consultants who enjoy (or tolerate) the marketing aspects, there is one more challenge or dilemma: While you're delivering the services you sold, you're too busy to do your marketing. Yet, when you finish your current assignment, where will your next job come from?

This dilemma is heightened because most marketing efforts have a long "incubation time"—often 3–12 months between successful sales calls and the first assignment.

Then, if you succeed at your first assignment, you may get more work right away. Or it could be a long time. Or never.

Selling (See SPIN® Selling in another section) can be more relaxed if you are in no hurry to develop your business (and income). Selling sometimes takes care of itself after operating for two to three years; your reputation and performance get known. You may be able to sign up a handful of corporate clients on a retainer basis, committing a few days a month to each one.

### Using Your Contact Network

Your contact network is the same marketing tool that works for 70–80% of the executives seeking new jobs; they are also selling themselves. And they use their contacts, primary and secondary, to gain a direct introduction and access to the decision-makers and gather inside information on a prospective client company's needs.

This will be your primary marketing approach—personal calls on decision-makers who have been introduced through a mutual acquaintance. This does not discourage cold calls, emails, direct mail, social media, or other marketing devices. But consulting is a word-of-mouth and performance-oriented market. Referrals from satisfied clients are like gold.

## Approaching the Network

If contacts are so effective, why do most executives avoid them? The reason is that people shy away from asking favors of friends and business acquaintances. If we transform the phrase "asking favors" into "seeking advice," we are changing the frame of reference into something far more acceptable to everyone concerned. The emphasis is on seeking advice and guidance from people whose judgment and opinion are respected and highly valued. Avoid giving the impression that you are asking these people for a job or contract. That may be your chief motive for talking to them, but this direct approach may push your contacts into a corner and generate antagonism, which is the opposite of what you want. What you want is a friendly hand up the ladder of success.

## Building the Network

You start building your network by listing all the influential people you know, for instance:

- Colleagues, past and present, and previous executives you worked for

- College classmates, professors, placement officers

- Professional acquaintances: lawyers, stockbrokers, bankers, accountants, real estate brokers, church leaders, insurance agents, members of Congress, etc.

- Fellow members of clubs or associations, neighbors, local merchants

- Officials of professional organizations, whether you are a member or not

- Participants in professional meetings you have attended or plan to attend

- Suppliers, previous customers, even your creditors

- Editors and writers of trade journals

- Family members and friends

Most executives can develop a list of 25 to 50 names at first. As time goes by, this number will gradually increase to a larger and larger group. Each of these names has a network of its own. One of your primary objectives is to link up with these other networks.

## Expanding the Network

The above list represents your primary contacts, the people you know directly and personally on at least a casual basis. Except for colleagues and former colleagues, there seldom are people who can offer you a job instantly. Instead, they become part of your communications system, which, after all, is your contact network and a means for expanding that system. Once you arrange an interview with your primary contact, the next step is to secure at least one or two other connections. This helps you start expanding your contacts indefinitely.

In developing your secondary contacts, it is essential to control the developing connection. Even if your primary contact offers to send your résumé or bio and credentials to other executives on your behalf, you must establish a method for following up yourself. If you do not retain the new contact's name, you lose control of the situation and have no assurance that the connection will be followed up.

## Six Marketing Techniques

There are still other methods for increasing your contact network and marketing yourself. We will now discuss six of these.

### Lectures

One of the most effective ways of meeting people is going on the lecture circuit. Most people are immediately impressed by individuals upon a platform. Speakers have the aura of public figures. If they have something interesting to say, it is much better. As you will undoubtedly have observed at the lectures you attended as a listener, many people cluster excitedly around the speaker after they have finished the talk. When speaking yourself, it would be advisable to have a handout—perhaps no more than an announcement of the lecture with your name, address, and phone number on it—that can serve as a memory aid for your listeners. If you subtly let it be known that you are also a consultant, some of your listeners may contact you as potential clients.

You can lecture before many groups, as long as you adjust your talk to your audience. You can give a speech to:

- Trade, technical, and professional societies

- Business, civic, and community groups

- Fraternal organizations, such as Kiwanis, Rotary, or Lions

### Directories

Another way of getting people to know you are to be listed in directories, especially the directories of the organizations for which you might lecture. Some of these may charge a fee or require a "contribution" of a significant sum, so use some care. It would help if you also considered setting up a personal website with links to social media: Instagram, Facebook, Twitter, and LinkedIn.

### Journal Articles

Another effective way to build a reputation as a consultant is to publish articles in trade journals and magazines in your field and post them online via LinkedIn and a blog. You probably already know many of them, but there may be others in related fields that you are not aware of. As with lecturing, you may also get paid for your effort.

### Newsletters

If you are skilled in writing, publishing a newsletter may be worth the cost. In the newsletter, you could discuss some of the interesting problems you are faced with as a consultant or the latest developments in your field. The newsletter would be for distribution to potential clients and should be written to engage their interests and hold their attention and make them aware of you as a consultant without seeming too much of a piece of self-promotion.

You could do this perhaps by having a regular column under your byline with a brief biographical note, somewhat like "Joe Smith, President of Market Research Consulting Service." You can reduce your cost by making the newsletter in blog form or email blasts.

### Professional Societies and Public Meetings

If you are uncomfortable speaking in public before large gatherings or writing essays, you might consider participating in trade, technical, or professional societies and various civic groups. This can be an effective way to meet influential people who can perhaps help you.

### Conduct Workshops or Seminars

In a workshop or seminar, you can get others talking and guide the discussions in the direction you are interested. It generally does not require an aggressive public presence. Many places might be interested in sponsoring you or at least providing you with space: colleges, churches and synagogues, community centers, the meeting halls of fraternal organizations, and so forth.

## CHAPTER SUMMARY

## Consultant Careers

Initially, joining an established corporate consulting firm is a good idea. You get a chance to learn what consulting is all about. You get the support of a group. And you have a climate wholly different from a giant corporation: more autonomy, less structure, more individual performance. If you decide later you can fly alone, you can still go that route, ensuring that you separate cleanly and honorably from your employer.

Another option is to become a consultant to your ex-employer, at least for a while. This works if they need you for specific knowledge and expertise. You have to back away from meddling in your former management role. You can also become an internal consultant in a large firm that has a group in human relations, training, or industrial engineering

To be a successful entrepreneur consultant, know yourself and your capabilities—interests, energy level, time limitations, selling, and delivery. Know your dollar situation. You need to carry yourself for one year or more. Assume zero income, many blind avenues, and first assignments do not necessarily pay well. It will probably be necessary to cut the price to get a foot in the door and build a client list. Typically, consultants are hired for specific needs and expertise that companies can't afford to keep on staff. Figure out your unique specialty, then match with companies who might need it. Network to find out where the need is using "informational interviews." Develop a marketing plan and start executing it.

## QUICK QUIZ

1. What is the difference between a consultant and a contractor?

2. What are the three main consultant career paths?

## QUICK QUIZ ANSWERS

1. What is the difference between a consultant and a contractor?

   - A consultant's role is to evaluate a client's needs and provide expert advice and opinion on what needs to be done

   - A contractor's role is generally to assess the client's needs and perform the work

2. What are the three main consultant career paths?

   - Entrepreneur consultant

   - Corporate consultant

   - Internal consultant

## DISCUSSION QUESTIONS

- What are the significant differences between the three types of consultants?

- What do you see as the significant challenge for an entrepreneur consultant?

## KEY TERMS

**External consultant:** Someone external to the client organization who can be contracted to conduct an evaluation and give expert advice. There are two primary careers categories for external consultants:

- Corporate (e.g., McKinsey & Company, Accenture)

- Entrepreneur (self-employed or small partnership)

**Internal consultant:** Someone who operates within an organization but is available to be consulted on areas of their specialization by other departments or individuals (acting as clients).

## END NOTES

The number one benefit that consultants can offer businesses is that they can provide temporary expertise. In addition, hiring a consultant allows firms to pay only for the services they need, rather than investing in pricey technologies or paying to keep staff on hand that may not always be required.

## REFERENCES

Block, Peter. *Flawless Consulting: A Guide to Getting Your Expertise Used.* Austin, TX: University Associated, 1981.

Holtz, Herman. *How to Succeed as an Independent Consultant.* New York: John Wiley & Sons, 1988.

Shenson, Howard L. *Complete Guide to Consulting Success.* Wilmington, DE: Enterprise Publishing, 1991.

Weinberg, Gerald M. *The Secrets of Consulting: A Guide to Giving & Getting Advice Successfully.* New York: Dorset House, 1985.

Small Business Administration. Small Business Readiness Assessment, 2022. https://eweb1.sba.gov/cams/training/business_primer/assessment.htm

## CREDIT

## CHAPTER 3

# Communicating with the Client

**LEARNING OBJECTIVES**

After reading this chapter, students will be able to do the following:

- Determine the communication style of the consultant.

- Determine the communication style of the consultant's clients.

- Develop a strategy to persuade the client to accept other consultants' ideas.

## Introduction

### Know Yourself and Know Your Client

Communication styles (e.g., personality types, temperaments) have gone by various names over the years. The theory has its roots in the ancient four humors theory. Some think its origin may have been in ancient Egypt or Mesopotamia. The Greek physician Hippocrates (460–470 BC) incorporated the theory into his medical views. Recently, the styles/types have been rediscovered.

For more than 75 years, psychologists have known that each of us has a recognized habitual communication style. The famous Swiss psychologist Carl Jung divided these styles into four classic types:

- Feeling: amiable; heart,

- Thinking: analytical; head,

- Sensation: driver; hands,

- Intuition: expressive; spirit.

Other sources may call these styles different names: Feeler, Thinker, Sensor, and Intuitor.

Each person has one of these as their dominant style (70% of the characteristics). Interestingly, as you get older, you become more of your dominant style (from 70% to 95%).

It is important to know our style; the client's communication style is equally essential. By understanding the characters of each style and how to determine the client's style, you can adapt to the client's style. This will dramatically improve your communication and understanding of the client. This adaption will improve the chances of selling your ideas to them. In addition, it improves your rapport with them. In the following few sections, we will learn the distinctions of the different styles, how to determine the client's style, and how to adapt our style to theirs.

We use the client's style as an important input to planning the opportunity interview for a consulting assignment. The key to the meeting is **listening, listening, listening**. Ask good questions based on the SPIN® meeting plan. The meeting flow consists of four primary phases: Preliminaries, Investigation, Demonstrating Capability, and Obtaining Commitment. The objective is to obtain information for defining the client's problem.

## Styles

### Which Style Are You?

There are four styles. These are shown in the Illustrations to the right and go by different names:

- Style 1 is also called Innovative and Heart, symbolized as Lassie;

- Style 2 is also called Analytic and Head, symbolized as an owl;

- Style 3 is also called Common Sense and Hands, symbolized as a wolverine; and

- Style 4 is also called Dynamic and Spirit, symbolized as a beaver.

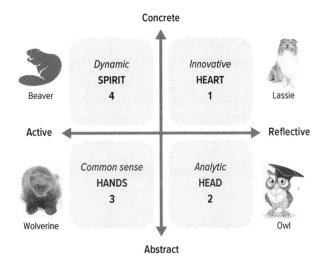

FIGURE 3.1  Four communication/thought processing styles

As we detail the styles, it will become more apparent why they go by these names and symbols. You and your client will be predominantly one of these styles.

The styles are always shown in the format below, with Style 4 and Style 1 on top and Style 3 and Style 2 below it.

### People-Oriented Styles

The people-oriented styles in the figure to the right are the top two styles (Styles 4 and 1). People with these styles share specific characteristics:

- People energize them

- They like physical touch (hugging)

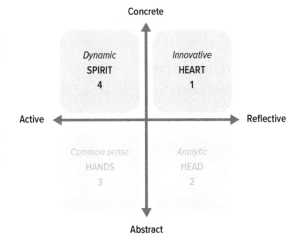

FIGURE 3.2  People-oriented styles

- They are right-brain oriented

- They are open and optimistic

- Good at giving affirmation

- See the big picture

- Viewed as naive at times

- They are perceivers and notice things that escape others.

## Task-Oriented Styles

The bottom two styles (4 and 2) in the illustrations to the right are the task-oriented styles. People who have these styles share specific characteristics:

- They are number oriented and analytical

- They see the parts (the trees, not the forest)

- Negative oriented

- Left-brain oriented

- Keep their distance

- Money is a significant motivator/driver

- They are de-energized by people

- See or notice something that is not very clear or obvious.

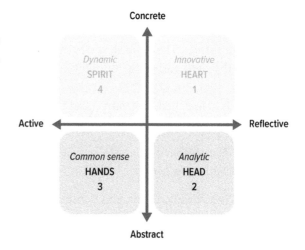

FIGURE 3.3  Task-oriented styles

## Action-Oriented Styles

The left two styles in figure 3.4 (4 and 3) are action oriented

- They act before they think

- They often seem to go "ready-fire-aim"

- Doing is all-important

- Tend to be spontaneous.

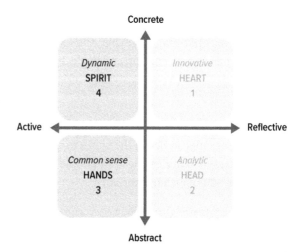

FIGURE 3.4  Action-oriented styles

## Thinking-Oriented Styles

The right two styles in figure 3.5 (1 and 2) are thinking oriented:

- They think before they act
- They will never shoot from the hip
- Employ careful consideration before taking action.

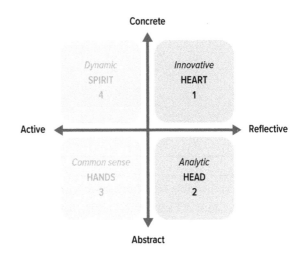

FIGURE 3.5  Thinking-oriented styles

# Quick Quiz 1

## What Is Your Style?

Circle Yes or No.

1. Are you a people-person?

   **a.** People **_energize_** you?                              Yes        No

   **b.** Enjoy being hugged or touched?                   Yes        No

   **c.** An optimist and positive person?               Yes        No

   Total # of circled items for Question 1. (Y/N)       _____   _____

2. Do you act before you think?

   **a.** Action oriented, _"Ready-Fire-Aim"_?            Yes        No

   **b.** Tend to be spontaneous?                              Yes        No

   **c.** A risk-taker?                                               Yes        No

   Total # of circled items for Question 2. (Y/N)       _____   _____

From the question totals above:

If Question 1 has more Yes than No, select Y under the Question 1 column below; otherwise, choose N.

If Question 2 has more Yes than No, select Y under the Question 2 column below; otherwise, choose N.

In the row that has both of your answers circled, the style in that row is **your style**.

| Question 1 | Question 2 | Then My Style is |
|:---:|:---:|:---:|
| Y | N | 1. Heart |
| N | N | 2. Head |
| N | Y | 3. Hand |
| Y | Y | 4. Spirit |

Based on the table selection above, circle Your Style. Also, circle your square in Figure 3.6. This is your predominant style (70% characteristics of you).

Knowing your style is key to understanding your natural way of communicating and thinking about things. Details of the styles can be found in the next section. First, the consultant must learn client's style. Then, the consultant adapts their style to the client's to maximize influence and improve rapport to understand their needs better. Consultants will learn how to determine the client's style in a later section.

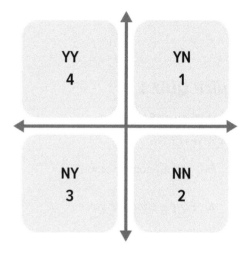

FIGURE 3.6  Determining your style

## Summary of Communication Styles

There are four basic communication styles. A summary description of each type is detailed below.

### Style 1: Heart

"Why Change?" "Let's work together!" "Let's keep things the way they are."

- Their environment includes family pictures, slogans on the wall, personal items, relaxed, friendly decorations

- They gain security through close relationships

- Their pace is slow and easy

- Their needs are a climate that administers

- They are irritated by pushy and aggressive behavior, insincerity, being put on the spot, disrupting the status quo

- For growth, they need to take risks, delegate to others, confront, develop confidence in others, learn to change and adapt

- Avoid conflict, sudden unplanned risky changes, overloading, confusing

How to relate:

- Wants you to be cooperative and pleasant

- Provide them with assurances, information on how it will affect their circumstances, popular ideas, risk sharing, reliability, and assistance in presenting to others

- General strategies: Be nonthreatening and sincere, show personal interest and support their feelings, don't push, move along slowly, show that you are listening, be easygoing, and assure them that you stand behind any decisions

Characteristics of Style 1:

| Positive | Negative |
|---|---|
| Sensitive feelings | Easily hurt |
| Loyal | Misses opportunities |
| Calm, even-keeled | Lacks enthusiasm |
| Not demanding | Weakling; pushover |
| Avoids confrontations | Misses honest intimacy |
| Enjoys routine | Stays in a rut |
| Dislikes change | Not spontaneous |
| Warm and relational | Few deep friends |
| Gives in | Codependent |
| Accommodating | Indecisive |
| Cautious humor | Overly cautious |
| Adaptable | Loses identity |
| Sympathetic | Holds on to others' hurts |
| Thoughtful | Can be taken advantage of |
| Nurturing | Taken advantage of |
| Patient | Crowded out by others |
| Tolerant | Weaker convictions |
| Good listener | Attracted to hurting people |
| Peacemaker | Holds personal hurts inside |

### *Style 2: Head*
"Do it right!" "Prove it!" "How was it done in the past?"

- Their environment is structured and organized, with charts and graphs, functional decor, formal seating arrangements

- They gain security by preparation

- Their pace is slow and systematic

- Their needs are a climate that describes

- They are irritated by people who do not know what they are talking about, lack of attention to detail, surprises, unpredictability

- For growth, they need to make faster decisions, tolerate conflicts, learn to compromise, adjust to change and disorganization

- Avoid criticizing, blunt personal questions, incomplete or inaccurate recommendations

How to relate:

- Wants you to be accurate and precise

- Provide them with evidence, information on how they can logically justify, systematic plans, progress reviews

- General strategies: Be thorough and well planned, support their thoughtful approach, demonstrate through action rather than words, be exact, organized, and prepared, give them time to verify your words, don't rush decision-making, avoid gimmicks, and provide evidence that what you say is true and accurate

Characteristics of Style 2:

| Positive | Negative |
| --- | --- |
| Reads all instructions | Afraid to break rules |
| Accurate | Too critical |
| Consistent | Lacks spontaneity |
| Controlled | Too serious |
| Reserved | Stuffy |
| Predictable | Lacks variety |
| Practical | Not adventurous |

| Positive | Negative |
|---|---|
| Orderly | Rigid |
| Factual | Picky |
| Conscientious | Inflexible |
| Perfectionist | Controlling |
| Discerning | Negative on new opportunities |
| Detailed | Rarely finishes a project |
| Analytical | Loses overview |
| Inquisitive | Smothering |
| Precise | Strict |
| Persistent | Pushy |
| Scheduled | Boring |
| Sensitive | Stubborn |

### Style 3: Hands
"Do it now!" "What's the point?"

- Their environment includes lots of projects, awards on the wall, a large calendar, office furniture arranged in a formal way
- They gain security by control
- Their pace is fast and decisive
- Their needs are a climate that responds
- They are irritated by wasted time, unpreparedness, arguing, blocking results
- For growth, they need to appear less critical, respect people's personal worth, develop a tolerance for conflict, pace themselves
- Avoid attacking their character, telling them what to do, presenting win-lose scenarios

How to relate:

- Wants you to be efficient and to the point
- Provide them with options, information on what it does and by when, freedom to act, immediate action

- General strategies: Be efficient and competent, support their goals and objectives if you disagree, argue facts and not personal feelings, be precise, time disciplined, well organized, focus on the results or bottom line, do not waste their time, let them make the decision

Characteristics of Style 3:

| Positive | Negative |
| --- | --- |
| Likes authority | Too direct or demanding |
| Takes charge | Pushy; can step in front of others |
| Determined | Overbearing |
| Confident | Cocky |
| Firm | Unyielding |
| Enterprising | Takes big risks |
| Competitive | Cold-blooded |
| Enjoys challenges | Avoids relations |
| Problem solver | Too busy |
| Productive | Overlooks feelings; do it now! |
| Bold | Insensitive |
| Purposeful; goal driven | Imbalanced; workaholic |
| Decision-maker | Inconsiderate of others' wishes |
| Adventurous | Impulsive |
| Strong-willed | Stubborn |
| Independent; self-reliant | Avoids people |
| Controlling | Bossy; overbearing |
| Persistent | Inflexible |
| Action oriented | Unyielding |

### Style 4: Spirit

"Trust me!" "Lighten up!" "It'll work out!" "Let's look at the future!"

- Their environment is cluttered and friendly, with awards and slogans on the wall, personal pictures

- They gain security by flexibility

- Their pace is fast and spontaneous

- Their needs include a climate that collaborates

- They are irritated by too many facts, too much logic, monotonous tasks, the same old approach, routine, being alone, ignoring their opinions

- For growth, they need to respect priorities, have a more logical process, follow-through, get better organized, concentrate on the task at hand

- Avoid negativism, rejection, arguing

How to relate:

- Wants you to be stimulating and interesting

- Provide them with quality information on how it will enhance their status, increased talent, originality, uniqueness

- General strategies: Be interested in them, support their dreams, feelings, and opinions, be sociable, do not hurry the discussion—give them a chance to verbalize, try not to argue, don't deal with details—put it all in writing, do not be shy, agree on the specifics of any arrangement

Characteristics of Style 4:

| Positive | Negative |
| --- | --- |
| Enthusiastic | Overbearing |
| Takes risks | Dangerous |
| Visionary | Daydreamer |
| Motivator | Manipulator |
| Energetic | Impatient |
| Very verbal | Attacks under pressure |
| Promoter | Exaggerates |
| Friendly, mixes easily | Shallow relationships |
| Enjoys popularity | Too showy |
| Fun-loving | Too flippant; not serious |
| Likes variety | Too scattered |

*(Continued)*

| Positive | Negative |
|---|---|
| Spontaneous | Not focused |
| Enjoys change | Lacks follow-through |
| Creative; goes for new ideas | Too unrealistic; avoids details |
| Group oriented | Bored with "process" |
| Optimistic | Doesn't see the details |
| Initiator | Pushy |
| Infectious laughter | Obnoxious |
| Inspirational | Phony |

## What Is the Client's Style?

Identifying the client's style and adapting to it in communications is key to influencing clients or winning a project proposal. There are many clues to help identify the client's style. Let's look at clues for each style.

FIGURE 3.7   What style is the client?

### Client Style 1: Innovative/Heart Clues

- The dress is typically comfortable and colorful: a bright tie, shirt, or colorful blouse.

- The office is comfortable, maybe neat, but usually messy. Family pictures will probably dominate the desk or wall.

- The person is warm and friendly, a "hugger." Those with Style 1 love people and interact with them. They are often apologetic in many ways (e.g., ordering food: "can I or may I have a …" instead of "I would like to have a …"). Most Style 1 people are likely to be overweight. It is not unusual for a Style 1 to touch your arm or hand during a conversation. To a Style 1, identifying with you is significant.

- Orientation is the past!

- Telephone clues:

  - Usually wants to talk

  - Reflecting, time to think

- Will often say "see"

- Uses "I" or "me" often

- Gives poor directions

- Not good with numbers

- May be interested in you as a person

## Client Style 2: Analytic/Head Clues

- The dress will be sharp, conservative with everything matching; well dressed.

- The office will be in order, with a clean desk. It will be a conservative, if not formal, setting. Diplomas and awards will be displayed on the wall. You can gain points by recognizing their accomplishments.

- The person is on time for appointments and expects that of you. Those with Style 2 are pretty serious; they talk directly, are straightforward, and expect verifiable facts presented to them. Style 2 clients are usually trim, seldom overweight.

- Orientation is the present!

- Telephone clues:

  - Follows proposal—page by page

  - Gives excellent directions

  - Reflecting, time to think

  - Asks lots of questions

  - Very interested in costs

  - Listen for pessimistic words

## Client Style 3: Common Sense/Hands Clues

- The dress will be stylish and carefully color-coordinated. The Style 3 usually has good taste, but sometimes tastes are exaggerated. Evidence may be way-out designs in clothing and excessive jewelry.

- The office is partly chaotic but somewhat orderly. It may be dominated by gadgets and the latest computer/iPad. The walls will have many pictures related to projects, awards, and trophies. The Style 3 client is the hands-on type who enjoys buying, owning, and using the latest inventions!

- The person will be image-conscious, reflected in the vehicles they drive, Apple watch, etc. Their eyes are often intense and intimidating. Their attitude is "I will win and on my terms." However, they can be very charming.

- Orientation is the now!

- Telephone clues:

  - Will it solve my problem?

  - Listen for extremes

  - Active, doesn't reflect

  - Can they win?

  - May be rude

  - Often thinks/says, "What's in it for me?"

## Client Style 4: Dynamic/Spirit Clues

- The dress is often sloppy—not important to Style 4.

- The office will be cluttered with stacks of books and papers everywhere: on the floor, window sills, and desks. You will never see a Style 4 with a clean desk. Instead, family pictures, outstanding awards, and plaques will adorn the walls and cabinets.

- The person is usually at ease with everyone, including strangers. Personal relationships are import-ant. Expect the conversation to flow easily.

- Orientation is the future.

- Telephone clues:

  - Needs to know potential

  - Is it simple to operate/use?

  - Active, doesn't reflect

  - Will it help me keep moving?

  - Usually will talk fast

  - Prefers a face-to-face encounter

# How to Communicate More Effectively with a Particular Style

The consultant must adapt to the client's style for effective communication. You learned in the previous section, how to identify the client's style. Use the following for tips for the client's particular style to influence them and selling your ideas and services to them.

## Client Style 1: Innovative/Heart

Phrases that will elicit interest and attention:

- People on your staff will like the way …

- William Jones, over at the IT Department, also thinks this is a good approach …

- Let's get reacquainted before we get down to business …

- Why don't we talk about this over lunch?

**Allow for small talk.** Remember that a Style 1 determines their attitudes about you and your ideas through their emotions. Small talk allows the Style 1 to evaluate the "vibes" between you and them. Do not begin the business part of your meeting until the Style 1 gives you a clue to start. For example, a Style 1 will often comment, "Well, what can I do for you today?"

**Explain how your proposal or idea can have a positive impact on others.** Show the relationship between your recommendations and their impact on people.

**Show how your idea has worked well in the past.** Whenever possible, show the traditional basis of what you are presenting. Remember, the time frame for the Style 1 is the past.

**Indicate how others react.** The Style 1 will respond favorably if individuals they know and respect also think well of your suggestions and ideas.

**Use an informal writing style.** When writing or emailing to a Style 1, be informal, opening and closing with a personal comment. The best way is to write as if you were speaking face-to-face.

**Avoid** conflict and confusing information.

## Client Style 2: Analytic/Head

Phrases that will elicit interest and attention:

- Let me walk you through the proposal, step by step …

- Before we start, let me bring you up-to-date …

- Let's look at this in a logical, systematic way …

- Why don't you study it over, and I'll get back to you …

- I have several alternatives for you to look at …

**Be precise.** Avoid such phrases as "generally speaking ...," or "it would appear that ...," or "approximately ...," etc. Where it is not possible to be precise, state ranges ("10 to 25%") or probabilities ("40% of the time ... will happen"). Also, all facts must be verifiable; e.g., what is the source?

**Organize your presentation.** One possible format for the organization would be chronological order. Tell what led up to the situation, what is evident at present, and what the outcome is likely to be. Another organizational scheme would be outline form. Break down your recommendations, ideas, or proposal into steps or phases. It is significant to a Style 2 to hear, "This project has three parts: a, b, and c. Let's go through it step by step."

**Include alternatives.** A statement that rapidly turns off a Style 2 is "I've got it all worked out, and here is the answer." It is all right to recommend a course of action, but the Style 2 likes to know you have considered other alternatives. For example, you might say, "There are three approaches we can take. I recommend Approach A, but here are the pros and cons of Approaches B and C for you to review."

**Do not rush a Style 2.** Most of them want to think things through. So when a Style 2 says, "I'd like to study this for a while," it is often not a stall but a genuine need to study and think about the idea.

**Outline your proposal.** When writing to a Style 2, outline form is most appropriate, using sub-indentations of 1, 2, 3 and a, b, c.

**Avoid** criticism and personal questions.

## Client Style 3: Common Sense/Hands

Phrases that will elicit interest and attention:

- We can get on it immediately.

- This will have almost immediate pay out.

- Suppose I skip the details and just hit the highlights.

- We tried to select the most practical approach we could find.

- This is "state-of-the-art"—the Style 3 loves status symbols.

- I only need five minutes of your time.

- I have a scale model (picture, graph, etc.) for you to look at.

**Indicate the results or conclusions first.** The Style 3 has neither time nor interest to wade through how you arrive at your position. Instead, tell them the recommendations or findings and then determine whether they are interested in hearing more.

**Do not offer many alternatives.** The Style 3 will want to know your "one best recommendation." It is all right to indicate that you have considered many options, but your opinion is that alternative A is best.

**State the practicality of your ideas.** Indicate how your proposal will bring immediate tangible results.

**Use visual displays**. Remember, the Style 3 deals best with things they can touch, see, and feel. A graph often says as much as several pages. A replica or model of your idea or suggestion speaks volumes.

**Be brief** when writing or presenting to the Style 3. Be succinct. One page is best for proposals or letters. Those that are several pages long will most likely end up in a file of papers to be read; it may be a long time before the Style 3 gets to it. If your recommendation is complex and lengthy, attach it as an appendix. Limit your cover sheet/executive summary to one page and indicate the subject, the outcome, and your recommendation.

**Avoid** wasting time.

## Client Style 4: Dynamic/Spirit

Phrases that will elicit interest and attention:

- I have a unique approach for you.

- This will pay off even more in the future.

- Let me begin by first giving you an overview.

- This approach ties in nicely with your concept of ...

- This is quite innovative, something that has never been tried before.

- Let me tell you about some of the basic principles (or concepts) on which this was designed.

**Allow ample time.** The Style 4 frequently responds to an intuitive thought pattern by linking one thought with the next. Often, they seem to go off on tangents as their mind considers one idea after the other. Most Style 4 people do not place a high premium on immediacy, and they enjoy the speculation of thinking a problem through by using their imagination in a discussion.

**Be conceptual.** In your opening comments, try to relate the specific topic at hand to a broader concept or idea. For example, if you have a particular suggestion for saving money, you might say, "I know, Mr. Style-4-Name, that you are very concerned about improving your investment return. I have an idea that I think will contribute toward that concept."

**Stress uniqueness.** Try to mention something in your presentation about the uniqueness of your idea. The Style 4 client responds well to what is new, out of the ordinary, or creative. Saying something like, "Here is something unique that has never been tried before" would strike a responsive chord with the Style 4.

**Emphasize future value.** Relate the impact that your idea or recommendation might have on the future. For example, "This will pay off even more next year."

**Do not stint on words.** When writing or presenting to a Style 4, do not be afraid to use a lengthy text. A Style 4 reads a lot and will not be dismayed by extended presentations. However, it might be good to start your proposal by indicating something about the concepts or principles upon which your ideas, thoughts, or recommendations are built. In other words, start with a global, broad treatment and work toward the more specific.

**Avoid** negativism.

# Quick Quiz 2

## What Style? Quiz

1. The man comes out to the office area to greet you. You mention that Joe Doakes asked if he remembered him, and he brightens perceptibly. You follow him into a cheery office and note that he is a science fiction buff. He has several framed illustrations from the 1920s and 1930s publications on the wall over a glass case containing several imaginative "future" machine models collected over the years.

   What is his style? _____ (1, 2, 3, or 4)

2. George seemed to sound off at somebody every ten minutes. He was under a lot of pressure, and maybe part of it was that he didn't take the time to keep off other people's toes. He told it like he saw it and to hell with everybody's feelings. Or so it seemed. If you looked a little closer, you would realize that he aimed to get the work out. His unit had a higher production record than most. And he never stayed mad.

   What is his style? _____ (1, 2, 3, or 4)

3. You soon realize that the customer wants to see comparative model changes for the past five years and any other bits of information you can give him. So you rifle through your briefcase and serve up the comparative figures, prices—the works. He reviews the models and tells you he would like to study them, and he will get back with his decision.

   What is his style? _____ (1, 2, 3, or 4)

## Quick Quiz 2 Answers

### Answers to What Style? Quiz

1. Style 1: He likes people, has a warm, cheery office, and likes things from the past.

2. Style 3: George is not people oriented, is very focused on getting work out. He is straightforward and no-nonsense.

3. Style 2: Very detail oriented; likes charts and numbers and will not make a fast decision.

---

**CHAPTER SUMMARY**

Successful consulting comes down to our ability to communicate clearly, concisely, and to be understood by everyone. This isn't easy. We all communicate a little differently. For example, some people give short, straightforward responses to questions, while others might add a ton of detail. But understanding our communication style and the client's, then adapting to the client's style, will bring invaluable clarity into how to be heard (and how to hear what everyone else is saying).

Understanding the client's style lets us know how to approach communicating with them. It will make it much easier to sell our ideas and recommendations. It builds rapport and trust—"we are on the same page."

Adapting to the client's style helps us ask better questions during our opportunity interview, using the SPIN® approach to determine the client's needs.

## DISCUSSION QUESTIONS

1. Describe how useful knowing the client's communication style is to the consulting assignment.

2. How would you structure your discussion to influence a Style 3 client effectively?

## KEY TERMS

There are four styles that people use to communicate and process information.

**Style 1** is also called Innovative and Heart, symbolized as Lassie; people oriented; time frame is the past.

**Style 2** is also called Analytic and Head, symbolized by an owl; task oriented; time frame is the present.

**Style 3** is also called Common Sense and Hands, symbolized as a wolverine; task oriented; time frame is now.

**Style 4** is also called Dynamic and Spirit, symbolized as a beaver; people oriented; time frame is the future.

## END NOTES

The concept of communication styles has been around for many years. For example, Hippocrates in ancient Greece (460–470 BC) identified four basic personality types/styles.

For more than 75 years, psychologists have known that each of us has a recognized habitual communication/learning style.

Dr. Carl Jung divided personal styles into four classic types. Two were people oriented, and two were task oriented

At the heart of Myers-Briggs's theory are four preferences. Do you prefer to deal with: People and things (Extraversion, or "E") or ideas and information (Introversion, or "I"). Facts and reality (Sensing, or "S"), or possibilities and potential (Intuition, or "N"). Myers-Briggs's work is based on Carl Jung's work. The Myers-Briggs Type Indicator is one of the most popular personality tests globally.

## REFERENCES

Brownsword, Alan W. *It Takes All Types!* (Revised ed.). Baytree Publication, 1999.

McCarthy, Bernice. *The 4Mat System.* Barrington, IL: Excel, 1980.

Sheve, Jeanna, and Kelli Allen. *Understanding Learning Styles.* Shell Education, 2010.

Zacharias, Raye. *Styles and Profiles.* Raye Zacharias, 1991.

## CHAPTER 4

# Determine Client Needs

**LEARNING OBJECTIVES**

After reading this chapter, students will be able to:

- Understand how to conduct an opportunity interview using the SPIN® techniques.

- Develop an understanding of the client's situation, complexities, and the questions they want to answer or the problem they want to be solved.

## Introduction

The key to a consulting assignment is understanding the client's needs. This chapter will introduce a structured approach to uncovering and developing client needs. First, the opportunity interview is used to determine facts about the client: their situation, problems, and their needs.

### Set Up an Opportunity Interview

The first step in an opportunity interview (sales call) is planning the telephone call to set up the meeting. The purpose of the call is multifold:

- To schedule a date, time, and meeting location for the session (virtual or in person—this is best) (maybe alternative times/dates)

- To determine the style of the main person at the meeting

- To get a basic understanding or idea of their issue/problem

Review the style information in the last chapter on phone clues to help formulate questions to determine the client's style. Try to talk to the person who will be at the opportunity meeting. During the phone call, try to get as much information as possible to help develop an initial set of problems.

- What is the perceived problem?

- Whom does the problem impact?

- Why is solving the problem significant (reduce cost, increase revenue, improve quality, etc.)?

# The Opportunity Interview

## Perform the Opportunity Interview

The objective of the introduction call is to ask for and set up an opportunity interview. Remember, the introduction call should be planned for approximately five to ten minutes. If it goes longer, that is a good thing. However, it would help if you created a script to ensure you get as much information as possible in a short time (five to ten minutes) and ensure you don't forget anything. The information you gather in the call will provide critical data to plan the opportunity interview meeting.

Prepare for the interview based on information collected in the introduction call and research (website, news, etc.) on the client. Create an initial set of problems from the information gathered during the call. Develop a meeting plan using the SPIN® approach in Section. Use the information from the call to determine the situation on the meeting plan form (see Section). Based on the situation and other information from the call and research, brainstorm (see Chapter 14, Section 14.2) possible related problems and implications.

Review the Styles in Section on how to relate/influence a particular style to frame the questions and the approach to the meeting. By considering the client's style, you can develop a rapport quickly and improve your information gathering and potential relationship. The first few minutes of a meeting are critical. The client will have an impression of you within the first minute. It is difficult to change their perception of you after that first impression.

Create a script of your introduction and practice before you get to the meeting. "Winging it" is the route to failure and not getting the job or information you need. The mindset must always be "it is about the client/prospect, NOT you."

Some conversation starters are:

- Notice something nice …

- Pay a compliment …

- Ask an opinion about something current (NO religion or politics) …

- Look for common ground.

Create an agenda for the meeting (see Section 14.6 on meetings) and have a copy available for the client. Go over it briefly. The opportunity meeting is about understanding the client's needs. The agenda should include identifying the client member for follow-up and project communication, identifying all stakeholders, critical success factors (what does success look like?), in addition to SPIN® questions (next section).

# SPIN® Approach to Determining Client Needs

The **SPIN®** model is a questioning approach to uncovering and developing client needs. This questing approach or model reflects the skills needed to succeed at a sales/opportunity event. The model was validated by Huthwaite's analysis of 35,000 sales calls over 12 years. Huthwaite's model was based on a structured dialogue with the client to clarify their needs. The key was aligning sales behavior to buying behavior by performing a needs assessment.

The starting point of the client's decision-making process (to hire you or not) is when they recognize their explicit need. The client will not hire you to solve their problems without a perceived need. The consultant's job is to help clients identify their needs by asking questions in a structured dialogue (SPIN® model). Assisting the client to understand their needs goes through several stages, beginning with feelings of dissatisfaction and progressing to a clear perception of their need and the problem they want or desire to solve or take action on.

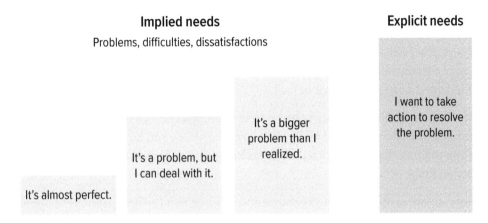

FIGURE 4.1  SPIN® model—implied, explicit needs

There are several stages (see Figure 4.1 above) to work through with the client to reach a shared understanding and clarity of their explicit needs. The more we develop the explicit need, the more likely the client will be ready to act and hire the consultant to solve their problem and satisfy their needs. The SPIN® model divides the client's needs into implied needs and explicit needs.

Implied needs are statements of problems, difficulties, or dissatisfaction in areas the consultant might be able to help.

Explicit needs are statements of the client's wants and desires to take action or solve the problem.

The consultant's job is to convert implied needs into explicit needs that the client is ready to take action on. This is achieved through the use of questions.

SPIN® stands for four types of questions:

- **S**ituation: Fact-finding questions to understand the present situation

- **P**roblem: Questions about client's difficulties

- **I**mplication: Questions about the effect of problems, and

- **N**eed-payoff: Questions about the value of the proposed solution.

During the lengthy "investigation" phase of any opportunity (sales) meeting, these questions come into play.

## Opportunity Interviews Flow

Opportunity interviews consist of four primary phases:

1. **Preliminaries.** Warming up the event at the start of the meeting. How are you? Nice weather? Is that a picture of your daughter? Did you catch that fish? Keep these questions and this phase short. One or two, and do not let them go on. You should use this stage to help determine the client's communication style. Hand out your business cards and ask the client for theirs.

2. **Investigation.** Finding out facts, information, and needs. How much do you see your company growing next year? How do you keep track of how much work your managers are accomplishing? What is your current work order system? Lots of time is spent in this phase. Here, you use the different SPIN° questions (more on that below).

3. **Demonstrating capability.** Showing you can solve their problem. You must resist going to this phase until the prospect has stated an Explicit Need for which you have a possible solution, such as, "I'm starting to think that a centralized CRM tracking system could help me keep track of my managers and vendors."

4. **Obtaining commitment.** Getting an agreement to proceed to a further stage of the opportunity. First, check that you have covered all of the client's (prospect's) key concerns. Then, help the client summarize the benefits of the project/engagement. Finally, propose the next appropriate level of commitment.

During the steps Investigation and Demonstrating Capability above, you use the SPIN° model and ask questions in a particular order:

- Situation

- Problem

- Implication, and

- Need-payoff.

After the meeting, create meeting minutes (see Section 14.7 on meetings) for your file. These notes will be vital to developing a proposal/Letter of Agreement to get the client's business. The illustration that follows shows how the SPIN® questions fit together.

## SPIN° Approach

Follow the flow (see Figure 4.2) and ask the questions in that order, realizing that depending on the client's answer, you may have to deviate occasionally.

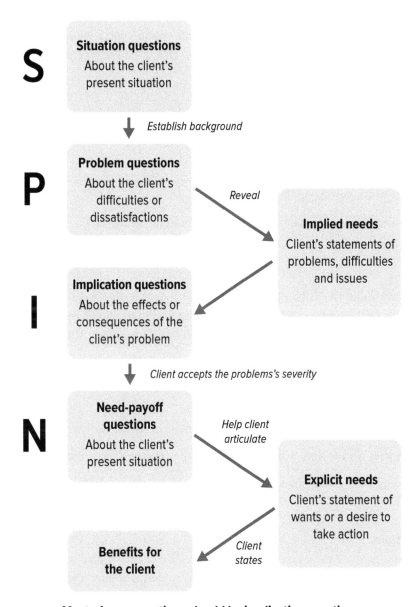

**Most of your questions should be implication questions.**

FIGURE 4.2  SPIN® approach to determining client needs

## SPIN® Question Definitions

Below is a summary of each type of question.

### Situation Questions

Situation questions are to get facts about the background of the client and what the client is doing. Do your research before the meeting to find answers to these questions. Situation questions bore the prospect. You may have to ask a few of them to find out or clarify the information you have researched on the internet. Use questions that will lead to asking problem questions. Use them sparingly. The questions should be targeted to the client's situation.

- Tell me about your company.

- How many customers do you have?

- Who are your major competitors?

- What type of software do you run here?

- Do you have multiple office locations that need access to the same data?

### Problem Questions

Problem questions are about the difficulties or dissatisfactions that the client is experiencing. Focus on this pain while clarifying the problem. These questions give rise to Implied Needs, which are the material for asking Implication Questions. Below are some examples (also, use them sparingly).

- Is it frustrating to lose sales to ABC Painting Supply?

- How easy is it to use your ERP system?

- How do you keep track of all your customer's phone calls between two offices?

- When someone goes on vacation, what happens to the properties they manage?

- What prevents you from producing a lower-cost product?

### Implication Questions

Implication questions are about the consequences or effects of a client's problems. This is the crucial line of questioning. Practice this skill often. Successful opportunity meetings contain many of these "implication" questions. The goal of using these questions is to persuade the customer to explicitly state a need that you can solve. You ask many of these questions to get the client to realize that they have a problem(s) that must be solved. Every business can be improved one way or another. The ultimate goal is to increase the client's perception of the value of our solutions. Implication questions are so vital that it's often helpful to break down the problems of a specific customer.

- What happens when your managers neglect the property owner's needs?

- Do you lose customers when people complain?

- Do you think it hurts your sales if you get lousy customer referrals?

- How much money do you lose when you lose a customer?

- How much does it cost you to get a new customer?

- What is the lifetime value of your customers, and how much will you make when you double it?

- Would you make more when your managers handled two more properties?

- How much does it cost you when three managers only work at 60% of your other managers?

- How long does it take you to find out who did what every day?

- How long do you spend going through old emails to find old communications?

- Will customers seek and demand better status reports?

- Do customers get frustrated by your service levels?


### Need-Payoff Questions

Need-payoff questions are about the value, usefulness, or utility the customer perceives in a solution. Like implication questions, need-payoff questions are strongly linked to success in the SPIN® model. Only ask these questions **after** the customer has confessed to a need or expressed an explicit need; otherwise, it **totally** fails because the customer can deny the existence of the need you claim to solve. You could use the questions below:

- How would it help if your offices were connected to a centralized database?

- Why is it important to get all your employees to account for their work?

- Would it be helpful if your homeowners made most of their requests without bothering anyone?

- Is there any other way that this could help you? Do you see the value in knowing which vendors do the most work?

After asking lots of questions and getting the client to admit to some explicit needs (not something vague), explain how your service solves the need. Demonstrating your capacity after the need is expressed brings the most success. Finally, attempt to address all prospective clients' concerns and ask them if they have any more problems. Next, ask the client to summarize the benefits of your service or proposed solution. Then, suggest the next appropriate level of commitment.


## Examples of Situations with Problem Questions and Follow-up Implication Questions

Below are several situations that a client may have. The examples give an example of possible problem questions and then the implied questions that could be asked. You should plan the opportunity interview at this level at a minimum.


### Situation 1: Offices in Different Locations

Problem: Cannot access the database from remote locations.

Implication questions:

- Do your vendors have to make extra trips to the office because they didn't have information locally?

- What happens when you need information about a customer in the evening and are at home?

- How many phone calls does your office take from customers looking for status updates on their problems? What would happen if you could reduce that number by 25%? Would that free up your receptionist's time by 25%, or could you hire 25% fewer customer support staff? What are the actual costs of a customer support representative, and how much do you save when they can do other tasks?

- When you are in another office and cannot access some pertinent information, does that cause a loss of efficiency?

- How do you know which office is more efficient? Who is in charge of making report evaluations about each office? How much time is spent on that?

Problem: High cost of maintaining IT infrastructure in multiple locations.

Implication questions:

- If a computer breaks in a remote office, do you have to send a support person out from the central office to fix it?

- Are your computer people in each office duplicating work that a central team could do?

- Is it difficult to get similar reports from different accounting and issue tracking systems?

### Situation 2: No Centralized Issue-Tracking Database
Problem: A manager cannot get information on a colleague's issues.

Implication questions:

- Do customers ever get frustrated when they call the office and no one has info on their problem?

- Do you ever find that important issues get dropped if a manager goes on vacation?

- Have you ever found a lot of duplicated effort when one problem gets reported multiple times?

Problem: Executives cannot monitor the performance of property managers.

Implication questions:

- If you cannot effectively monitor what is happening with each of your properties, have you ever had problems from issues that suddenly blew up?

- Have you ever suffered because one of your property managers was not performing, but you weren't aware of the problem?

## Call/Meeting Plan

You should prepare a Call/Meeting Plan (see the form in Figure 4.3) to prepare for the interview with the client. The Call Objective is what you expect from the call/meeting (e.g., a signed agreement, agreement to another meeting, information for a proposal, etc.).

The Situation section should highlight what we know about the client (e.g., multiple locations, multiple product/service lines, financial situation, etc.) and an initial problem statement.

The Problems and Implications section should be completed in the form like the examples above. Think about their current situation, the conversations you have had with the client, and the client research.

What are the problems you think they may want you to investigate or that you know similar companies have these problems in this area? For example, if they have problem x, what does that imply: additional overtime hours, quality issues, lack of proper data, or access to data?

| Call Plan | |
|---|---|
| **Call Objective** _Get in advance_ | |
| **Situation** _Further facts_ | |
| **Problems** _That are solvable_ | **Implications** _That increase seriousness or urgency_ |
| **Explicit needs** _That will be developed_ | **Benefits** _That can be offered_ |

FIGURE 4.3  Sample call plan form

## SPIN® Approach Review

Remember, the SPIN® approach asks questions in a particular order, as shown in the flow in Figure 4.4. Therefore, the client states the Explicit Need and the Benefits. They are essential information in developing the Problem Statement and Proposal, discussed in later chapters.

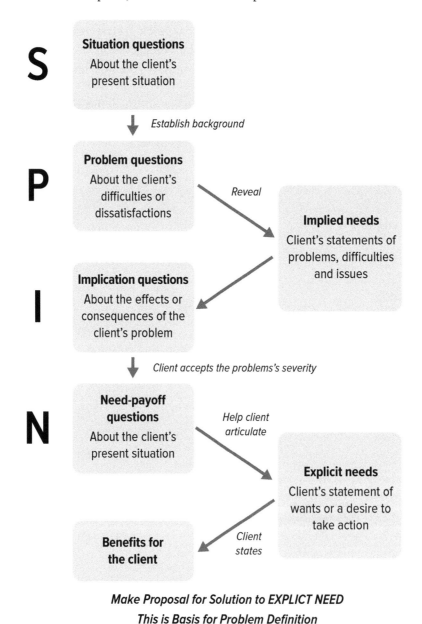

FIGURE 4.4 SPIN® approach review

# Opportunity Interview Closing

Review with the client all actions (e.g., items client will send you, items consultant will do or send client) agreed to during the interview. Also, restate the client's explicit need (Client Problem) and ensure everyone agrees.

Make sure you have covered the following items:

- Who the stakeholders are

- How the project communication approach is going to work

  - Client point person

  - Consultant point person

  - Status reports (to whom)

- Critical success factors and client expectations for the project

  - What do you not like about how need is currently addressed?

  - What do you want instead?

- Why is solving the problem significant (reduce cost, increase revenue, improve quality, etc.)?

  - Determine next steps for client and consultant (next meeting, etc.).

On your second meeting, you should create a "business model" of the client's business using data flow diagrams (see Chapter 14.3) or swim lanes to understand how the client's problem fits with the rest of their organization. The business models will bring clarity to the solution and what changes need to be made in the flow of business for the client.

Close the meeting.

Ensure that detailed notes (see Meeting in Chapter 14.7) are created for the opportunity interview. This gives the information for the next step, finalizing the agreed problem statement and documenting it via a proposal/Letter of Agreement (LOA).

**Send a thank-you email/note thanking them for their time and information.**

Remind them of the next steps. Ask the client if they are ready to proceed with the consulting engagement. If so, ask the client to send you an email asking for a Letter of Agreement to proceed.

## CHAPTER SUMMARY

Successful consulting comes down to our ability to communicate in a way that's clear, concise, and understood by everyone. This isn't easy. We all communicate a little differently. Some people give short, straightforward responses to questions, while others might add a ton of detail.

Adapting to the client's style helps us ask better questions during our opportunity interview. We use the SPIN° approach to determine the client's needs. The data we collect through this approach and process gives us the information to formulate the client's issue (explicit need) that they want a solution(s) to improve their operation.

We also determine the stakeholders, the project communication approach (i.e., status reports to whom), critical success factors, and expectations for the project. This gives us the information for the next steps, finalizing the agreed Problem Statement.

## QUICK QUIZ: NEEDS ASSESSMENT

1. Indicate whether each of the following is an implied (I) or explicit (E) need.

   a. We spend too much money on maintaining our system _____

   b. We need to reduce delays in our system _____

   c. We must find a better way to speed up turnaround time _____

2. Indicate whether each of the following is a situation (S) or problem (P) question.

   a. What is the average weekly output of this plant? _____

   b. Is it hard to recruit skilled people? _____

   c. Have you had any trouble controlling quality? _____

3. Indicate whether each of the following is an implication (I) or needs-Payoff (N) question.

   a. How has increased workload affected turnover in support staff? _____

   b. Would it be helpful if I could show a way to manage the increasing workload? _____

   c. Have these staffing problems led you to lose customers? _____

## QUICK QUIZ ANSWERS

1. Indicate whether each of the following is an implied (I) or explicit (E) need.

   a. We spend too much money on maintaining our system: I.

   b. We need to reduce delays in our system: E.

   c. We must find a better way to speed up turnaround time: E.

**2.** Indicate whether each of the following is a situation (S) or problem (P) question.

   **a.** What is the average weekly output of this plant? S

   **b.** Is it hard to recruit skilled people? P

   **c.** Have you had any trouble controlling quality? P

**3.** Indicate whether each of the following is an implication (I) or needs-payoff (N) question.

   **a.** How has increased workload affected turnover in support staff? I

   **b.** Would it be helpful if I could show a way to manage the increasing workload? N

   **c.** Have these staffing problems led you to lose customers? I

## DISCUSSION QUESTIONS

**1.** Describe the main idea of the SPIN° approach to determining a client's needs.

**2.** Describe how you know when the client has discovered his Explicit Need.

## KEY TERM

**SPIN®:** Stands for four types of questions: **S**ituation, **P**roblem, **I**mplication, and **N**eed-payoff. These questions are used during the lengthy "investigation" phase of any sales or need assessment meeting.

## END NOTES

Neil Rackham, *SPIN® Selling*, McGraw-Hill, 1988.

This is an absolute classic (initially published in 1987) as "Making Major Sales" shows through massive research how classic sales techniques fail miserably in big business and that you can get greater success by asking a sequence of Situation, Problem, Implication, and Need-Payoff questions.

Neil Rackham, *The SPIN® Selling Fieldbook: Practical Tools, Methods, Exercises, and Resources,* McGraw Hill, 1996.

*The SPIN® Selling Fieldbook* is about how to stop talking and start asking the right questions and listening. This is a hard-to-develop skill, and Rackham gives you step-by-step instructions to do it for your business, service, or product. In addition, the book demonstrates that I and N questions of implication and need-payoff are time well spent.

The SPIN® Selling Fieldbook is your guide to the method that has revolutionized big-ticket sales in the United States and globally. It's the method used by half of all Fortune 500 companies to train their sales forces. It is the interactive, hands-on fieldbook that provides the practical tools you need to put this revolutionary method into action immediately. *The SPIN® Selling Fieldbook* includes:

- Individual diagnostic exercises

- Illustrative case studies from leading companies

- Practical planning suggestions

- Provocative questionnaires

- Practice sessions to prepare you for dealing with challenging selling situations

Written by Neil Rackham, the pioneering author of the original bestseller, *SPIN® Selling*, this book makes utilizing the methods and techniques easy for a consultant.

## BIBLIOGRAPHY/REFERENCES

Becker, Hal B. *Can I Have 5 Minutes of Your Time*? The Becker Group, 1993.

Holtz, Herman. *How to Succeed As An Independent Consultant*. New York: John Wiley & Sons, 1988.

Rackham, Neil. *SPIN Selling*. New York: McGraw-Hill, 1988.

_____. *Major Account Sales Strategy*. New York: McGraw-Hill, 1989.

_____. *The SPIN Selling Fieldbook*. New York: McGraw-Hill, 1996

# Stakeholders

## Introduction

According to Machiavelli, "[T]he initiator has the enmity of all who would profit by the preservation of the old system and merely lukewarm defenders in those who would gain by the new one." And that is precisely what a consultant does when accepting an engagement to change the organization's operating environment. So, who are all these people in the organization that Machiavelli might be referring to? These are the stakeholders.

### Strategic Value of Engagement

Before getting too far into the processes relating to stakeholders of an engagement, it is prudent to understand the value that the engagement sponsor has attributed to the potential outcome of the engagement to the organization and to the various subdivisions within the organization.

The **sponsor** has determined a set of "values" before suggesting to the organization's management to start the engagement. Here is what those values might be:

FIGURE 5.1 Niccolò Machiavelli, 1513

- The value of the outcome to their division(s) of the organization consists of financial gains or operating efficiencies.

- The sponsor's management must have agreed to that value to allow the engagement to go forward.

- The perceived value that the sponsor has of the benefits to the other divisions within the organization.

- The sponsor's reputation.

So, moving forward, the consultant should understand the stakeholder's beneficial relationship with the engagement—or not.

This effort also implies that the sponsor has some "skin" in the engagement, which should benefit the consultant if deftly used.

### What Is a Stakeholder?

**Stakeholders** and the arena in which they operate may be financially, organizationally, and positionally affected by, or affect your engagement.

One way to characterize stakeholders is by their relationship to the engagement.

- **Primary stakeholders** are the people or groups that stand to be directly affected, either positively or negatively, by your engagement; in some cases, there are primary stakeholders on both sides of the equation: a change that benefits one group may harm another.

- **Secondary stakeholders** are people or groups indirectly affected by your engagement, either positively or negatively.

- **Tertiary stakeholders**, who might belong to either or neither of the first two groups, can positively or negatively affect an effort on who is vital within the organization in which you may have an engagement. These certainly could be the staff that either is involved in any outcomes of the engagement or could influence its success.

## How Do You Identify These Stakeholders?

During the initial meetings, when you determine the scope of the engagement, some questions should be asked to identify the stakeholders.

The following are a few examples:

- What would success look like to you? To your organization? Who else in your organization would see it this way?

- Where did the problem that we are discussing originate? Who would it impact if it were solved or wasn't?

- How ready is the organization to change to solve this question? Who supports these changes, and who might not?

- Has there been anyone else in the organization trying to solve this problem? Who are they? What was the outcome?

- What, in your opinion, is the root cause of this problem, where in the organization did it evolve, and who is involved? Have there been long-standing critics of this situation?

- What are the barriers to the success of this engagement? And where and who might be involved in erecting those barriers?

- Does anyone else in the organization have an interest in the outcome of this engagement? What do you think is their interest?

- Who have you consulted with who has formulated the parameters of this engagement?

- Who else would I be talking to?

- Who are the people who will be deciding on the success or failure of this engagement?

The answers to the above questions will give you the starting points to expand the potential list of stakeholders. Some variations on the above questions will allow you to expand the list.

## Benefits of Stakeholder Engagement

There are many benefits of stakeholder engagement:

- It offers those who will affect or be affected by the results a chance to voice their opinions

- It enables the consultant to identify who the stakeholders are and broadens the consultant's knowledge and understanding of the organization

- Allows the pooling of knowledge to understand interactivity better

- It helps reduce risk within an engagement by gaining complete information

### Analyzing Stakeholders

Why should you identify them and then analyze their place in the organization?

- It will add richness to the overall consulting effort—the more you know will add value to your recommendations.

- It adds perspective by giving depth to your investigations.

- It adds to the overall buy-in for the engagement.

- It will reduce the possibility of hearing phrases like "Why wasn't I told about this?" or "That is not how it works around here!" or "You don't understand the real problem that needs to be addressed."

- It fosters credibility for your consultancy and the engagement.

- It provides the consultant knowledge for suggesting future engagement opportunities!

## When Should You Identify and Analyze Stakeholders?

This process should be in the first echelon of activities performed. No one likes to be the afterthought and a latecomer to the engagement; they know that their input will have less or no impact on considerations for the final recommendations.

How do you evaluate the stakeholders' interests? First of all, stakeholders' interests will vary, depending on the following:

- Areas of responsibilities;

- Positions in those areas of responsibility;

- Positional or personal financial exposure; and/or

- Political impacts.

### Relevance of Stakeholders

All organizations are not created equal in size, wealth, complexity, or the impact of complex product structure or reliance on external materials, products, or services. Each of these factors can either complicate or simplify their importance. The consultant needs to make this judgment early in the engagement as it is an existential factor in the success of the engagement and the consultant's credibility.

In addition to the above, each identified stakeholder needs to be assessed as to the following characteristics:

- High interest, high influence to either support or cause mischief in the engagement.

- High interest and be of support to the engagement but has little power to influence it.

- Those who have great power but are marginally interested or involved.

- Sleepers have little interest and little power and may not even know the effort exists.

Once you have identified the stakeholders, you must assign one of the above classifications and whether they are harmful and oppositional or supportive and positive. Once you have determined the characteristics of the stakeholder, you need to act, and it is suggested that you develop a Stakeholder Action Involvement Matrix (Table 5.1) as seen below, as to how you will deal with them.

Suppose you have a negative/oppositional stakeholder. In that case, you must spend some time turning them into positive/supportive. If you cannot achieve either of these, then be prepared to deal with a potential conflict. The consultant should engage the sponsor in this effort, as the sponsor is interested in avoiding any conflict. But whether there is a conflict or not, there is value in their ability to add a better understanding of the organization.

The sponsor can be a very valuable and "interested" stakeholder—yes, the sponsor is a stakeholder and has excellent reasons to be an ally in working with the other stakeholders.

**TABLE 5.1    STAKEHOLDER MANAGEMENT**

| Stakeholder | Communication | Visits | Stake |
|---|---|---|---|
| | Status reports | Upon request | Areas of interest |
| | | | Areas of influence |
| | | | Areas of impact |

# Phase II

We have been explaining the processes to shepherd the engagement into and through its execution and to its final presentation of the engagement results. Everyone could love the engagement and the results, but perhaps some, not so much.

Before publishing the engagement results, it would be prudent to assess, with the sponsor, what each stakeholder's response could be. Then, for each stakeholder, the consultant should determine those who are impacted (consultant's and the sponsor's view):

- Positive impact: Financial, new opportunities, efficiency, or new responsibilities. Document them and relate the results to the objective of the engagement.

- Negative impact: Financial, lost opportunities, loss of efficiency, or loss of responsibilities. Document them and relate the results to the objective of the engagement.

The consultant and the sponsor (and management?) should decide how to handle the "negative" impacted stakeholders. There are two ways—before the public announcement or after. This is usually the organization's decision.

If there are no negative impacts, then congratulations.

## CHAPTER SUMMARY

The people in an organization with whom you are performing an engagement are crucial to successfully completing your engagement. The consultant will use these people to provide the information needed to uncover problems and formulate hypotheses to uncover the problems and develop a solution.

These people who are uncovered can be operatives or knowledgeable observers. However, some people are not operatives or knowledgeable observers but are impacted by the consultation findings.

All of these mentioned people are known as stakeholders, and they are all important in that they all can have a bearing on the success of the consultation. Some, however, may not have a positive view of the consultant's charge or results. These stakeholders need to be included within the process and educated on the effort's intent, process, and potential benefits.

An important stakeholder is the sponsor of the consultation, and that particular stakeholder is an important resource for the consultant to work their way through the consulting process.

## QUICK QUIZ

1. What one person would be the most important person that you could talk to at the beginning of the project?

2. Why?

3. Who is more important—the powerful stakeholder who is interested in the outcome of the engagement, or the sponsor?

## QUICK QUIZ ANSWERS

1. The manager of the sponsor, or the highest level of the organization that needed to approve the engagement.

2. To better understand the value of the engagement to the organization and understand the expectations of the outcomes. In addition, the consultant can understand the impact of the engagement results on that person's peers.

3. The sponsor. In concert with the sponsor, the consultant can work to change the perspective of the important stakeholder, but if unsuccessful, the lack of agreement could end up at the desk of the sponsor's management.

## DISCUSSION QUESTIONS

1. What is the sponsor's interest in the outcome of the consultancy?

2. Why might a key stakeholder have a negative feeling about the consultancy?

## KEY TERMS

**Sponsor:** The person responsible for the overall success of the project.

**Stakeholders:** Individuals and organizations who are actively involved in the project or whose interests may be positively or negatively affected as a result of project execution.

## END NOTES

The consultant must wear many hats in executing an engagement, and one of the most important is risk management. Knowledge in various areas of expertise is important as process and procedural tradecraft, but risk management is essential.

## REFERENCES

Everitt, Jessica. *How to Create the Perfect Stakeholder Management Plan, 2022.* https://www.wrike.com/blog/how-create-stakeholder-management-plan/.

Management Project. *Stakeholder Management, 2022.* https://www.projectmanager.com/guides/stakeholder-management

## CREDITS

# Define the Problem

## Introduction

Business problems can be wicked in nature:

• Ill-defined and unique

• Several critical unknowns

• Conflicting stakeholder views

• Too much or too little data

• Limited time and resources

• Interdependence

In science, you deal with "what is." In consulting, you deal with "what does not yet exist." This is what makes it necessary to have a structured approach to solving the business problem.

In the previous chapters, we learned to identify the client's style and how they process information. Then, we learned how to use this information to build rapport and gain influence. We also learned a structured needs assessment approach called SPIN®. We used this approach to find critical information about the client, his or her problems, the implication of those problems, and agreed explicit needs.

We will use the Minto method to help the client understand their explicit needs and the key question they want to be answered. We will use the information from the Minto diagram (described in the next section) as a starting point for developing the client's **problem statement** to define the framework, scope, and domain of the consulting engagement. After we get an agreement from the client that this is the problem they want to be solved, we can develop a Letter of Agreement (LOA) that will become the contract for proceeding with the engagement.

## Determine the Client's Problem (SCQ)

In the previous chapter, we determined the client's explicit need. The best way to express that need is a problem statement. The best way for the consultant to structure their thinking for developing a problem statement is to use the Minto approach to **SCQ**:

- Understand the client's **S**ituation

- Determine the **C**omplexities related to the situation

  - R1: What do we not like about it?

  - R2: What do we want instead?

- Develop the **Q**uestion that the client wants answered.

  - How do we get from R1 to R2?

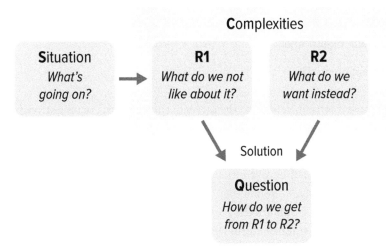

FIGURE 6.1  Using the Minto approach to structure thinking for developing a problem statement, flow chart

## Develop a Problem Statement

The problem statement defines the scope and domain of what the client wants to be answered. The problem statement will be the key to developing the letter of agreement (LOA) and conducting the consulting engagement.

## What Is a Problem Statement?

A problem statement clearly describes the client's problem you are trying to solve and is typically most effectively stated as a question. Clearly defined problem statements are critical in effective problem solving. Problem statements should be used at the beginning of any project to frame and focus the engagement. A good problem statement defines the "who" involved in the problem and defines the scope of the problem. Since the problem statement guides much of the problem solving of a project, it is essential not to be too narrow or broad. The easiest way for a project to get off track is if the consultant and the client are trying to solve different problems. A good problem statement aligns the client's expectations with the consultant's activities and deliverables. Finally, a problem statement frames an issue such that we know what success looks like.

### Use the Five Ws and One H

When developing a problem statement, the most useful tools are the five Ws and one H, which is who, what, why, where, when, and how to frame the problem statement.

- Who does the problem impact?

- What are the drivers of the problem?

- Why is solving the problem significant (reduce cost, increase revenue, improve quality, etc.)?

- Where does the problem reside?

- When did the problem begin? and

- How was the problem created?

  Thinking through these questions related to the problem can help you create a strong problem statement.

### Ask the Most Crucial Question: "What Are We Trying to Solve?"

The most effective question that can be used in a problem statement meeting/brainstorming session is simply, "What are we trying to solve?" Remember the Minto diagram. It cuts through the clutter, confusion, and misalignment and quickly centers the focus and energy. First, we should identify the unwanted result and the desired result. This will be helpful when we start dissecting the problem via issues analysis (detailed in the chapter 9) and helps us properly frame the problem.

### Characteristics of a Good Problem Statement

What are we trying to achieve? The basic question we are trying to solve. The problem statement should be SMART: **S**pecific, **M**easurable, **A**ction-oriented, **R**elevant (to the question), and **T**ime-bound.

- Background and context: What is the current situation? What has happened so far? Why is this problem being addressed now?

- What is success? What does an excellent final product look like? What are we trying to deliver?

- Stakeholders: Who are the decision-makers? Who needs to be involved?

- Potential challenges: What are the potential issues or problems we can foresee and plan to mitigate?

- Where will we find information and help? Where do expertise and knowledge exist (internal and external)? E.g., work that has already been completed by internal experts; we should draw on published reports and papers.

## Frame the Problem Statement as a Goal

Some of the best problem statements are simply goals formatted as questions. For example, if you need to increase performance by 15%, a good problem statement is, "Within the next 12 months, what are the most effective options for the client to increase performance by 15%?"

We must ask two important questions to frame a solution set:

- What can we do about the problem?

- What should we do about the problem?

## CHAPTER SUMMARY

In this chapter, we used all the information collected through meetings and discussions with the client, including information about the client, their issues and problems, and the kind of service they wanted. We developed a well-defined and precise problem statement that frames the consulting engagement.

The problem statement should answer the base question the client wants to solve. It should be SMART: specific, measurable, action-oriented, relevant, and time-bound.

We obtained the client's agreement that the documented problem statement is the correct one to solve. Then, we will send them a Letter of Agreement, after which signing the consultant will begin the project.

## QUICK QUIZ

Identify the components of a Minto diagram and approach to problem solving in the discussion below.

The HT Fitness Company (details in chapter 14.9) developed a dynamic and profitable business in only five years. HT Fitness has a loyal membership that uses the gyms regularly.

The gyms have strength machines and free-weight areas. Their membership is predominantly males, 35 to 45 years old. They are serious bodybuilders and strength-training amateur athletics. In recent years, the company has lost profits and membership has declined. HT Fitness would like to turn this situation around and increase its membership.

1. What is S (Situation)?

2. What is R1 (What is wrong)?

3. What is R2 (What is desired)?

4. What is the question?

## QUICK QUIZ ANSWERS

1. What is S (Situation): Fitness company with gyms that traditionally had serious 35-to-45-year-old male amateur athletes who make up the majority of its membership.

2. What is R1: (What is wrong): Losing membership.

3. What is R2: (What is desired): Increase membership.

4. What is the question: What is causing the drop in membership?

## DISCUSSION QUESTIONS

1. What is the best way to use the Minto approach for determining the problem statement?

2. Do you think it will help the client understand what they want to be solved?

## KEY TERMS

**Problem statement:** A clear description of the problem you are trying to solve, it is typically most effectively stated as a question. Problem statements are critical in practical problem solving. They have an uncanny ability to focus their efforts on brainstorming, teamwork, and projects.

**SCQ:** Understand the **S**ituation, determine the **C**omplication, formulate the key **Q**uestion

## END NOTES

**Minto Principle.** Consultants must structure their thinking. This is the best way to present your ideas clearly to clients. One excellent tool is the pyramid principle by an ex-McKinsey consultant by the name of Barbara Minto. She authored a book called The Minto Pyramid Principle, which essentially defined the way consultants structure most of their presentations. Most consultants will know the pyramid principle, even if they don't know the author.

The Pyramid Principle advocates that "ideas should always form a pyramid under a single thought." The single thought is the answer to the key question. Underneath the single thought, you are supposed to group and summarize the next level of supporting ideas and arguments.

## REFERENCES

Minto, Barbara. *The Pyramid Principle: Logic in Writing and Thinking.* Minto International, 1987.

Stareva, Iliyana. *8-Step Framework to Problem-Solving* from McKinsey, 2018. https://medium.com/@
IliyanaStareva/8-step-framework-to-problem-solving-from-mckinsey-506823257b48.

## CREDIT

## CHAPTER 7

# Develop a Letter of Agreement (LOA)

**LEARNING OBJECTIVES**

After reading this chapter, students will be able to:

- Document the approach, associated costs, and estimated timeline to develop the findings, recommendations, and solutions to meet the client's needs.

- Learn how to prepare a Letter of Agreement (LOA).

## Introduction

In the previous chapters, we learn to identify the client's style and how they process information. We also learned a needs assessment approach called SPIN®. We used this approach to find out information about the client, their problems, the implication of those problems, and agreed on possible solutions.

We use the information from the Minto diagram as a starting point for developing the client's problem statement. The problem statement is used to define the framework, scope, and domain of the consulting engagement. After we get an agreement from the client that this is the problem they want to be solved, we can now develop a **letter of agreement** (LOA) that will become the contract for proceeding with the engagement after both parties have signed.

## Letter of Agreement

The letter of agreement (LOA) is a contract between the consultant and a client who wants to secure their services. This agreement will serve as a legal document for both parties. It clearly defines what the consultant will do for the client on this particular engagement. The LOA should include terms that cover the consultant and the client, the terms of service, the compensation details, intellectual property rights, confidentiality, non-competition, and non-solicitation.

The LOA should have the following sections:

- Consultant: Basic contact information (name, address, phone number)

- Client: Basic contact information (name, address, phone number)

- Final statement of the problem and deliverables with details about services that the consultant will provide

- Client responsibilities and assumptions

- Compensation details: How much clients will pay, how they will be invoiced, late payment terms, etc.

- Governing law: Choose the applicable law (what state)

- Terms of service: Include details about how either party can terminate the agreement, timeframe of service

- Intellectual property rights: Who will own any work product created. Generally, any intellectual property built belongs to the client, but the consultant agreement can assign ownership rights to either party.

- Confidentiality: Terms that prevent a consultant from disclosing the company's confidential information, such as trade secrets, client lists, and other proprietary information

- Non-competition: Terms that prevent the consultant from directly competing with the client for a specific time

- Non-solicitation: Terms that prevent the consultant from soliciting customers or employees of the client without prior written consent

- Termination: If parties agree to a process for earlier termination of the agreement

- Entire agreement: Statement that this is the whole agreement between the parties

- Notices: Provide contact information and instructions on how to send any notifications (e.g., by registered mail, return receipt requested)

- Signatures: Statements such as, "In witness of whom, the parties agree …" followed by both parties' signatures.

The letter of agreement (LOA) will have an overall budget and timeframe. Finally, the LOA is submitted to the client for approval.

While we are awaiting the approval:

- We can start a staffing plan;

- What staff is available for what role;

- The timeframe for using a particular staff member;

- Finalize framing the project.

## Sample LOA

This Letter of Agreement ("Agreement") is entered into this 15th day of March 2022 ("Effective Date") by and between HT Fitness, Inc. (HTF, or "Company"), a Texas corporation with offices at 666 Ettu Lane,

Houston, TX 77777 and Roman Consulting Corporation ("Consultant"), located at 777 Main Street, Houston, TX 77666 for professional services to be provided to "Company" by "Consultant" subject to the terms and conditions of this Agreement.

1. Problem Statement: Should HTF change its focus on strength training to reduce membership losses?

2. Approach and deliverables:

   ▪ The Consulting firm's approach is to develop a set of hypotheses based on the problem statement and then use the consulting team's staff to prove these hypotheses.

   ▪ The Company will approve the chosen hypotheses before the Consultant begins the proof mode.

   ▪ This approach will be used to keep the cost of analyzing the problem and determining the solution(s) at a minimum.

   ▪ The cost is comprised of interviewing principals most familiar with the factors related to the hypotheses, research, and analysis to synthesize a set of recommendations.

   ▪ If the hypotheses are not proven to be the "right" hypotheses, then another set will be chosen and agreed to by the Company. The amount charged in this Letter of Agreement reflects the charge for the first hypothesis.

   ▪ Deliverables include findings and recommendations in PowerPoint format.

3. Scope of Services:

   ▪ Performing the work of defining the problem as seen by the Company.

   ▪ Performing the analysis of an issue.

   ▪ Formulating the hypotheses.

   ▪ Testing the hypotheses.

   ▪ Developing recommendations.

4. Company Responsibilities:

   ▪ The Company will make key staff available on a timely and as-needed basis and provide documentation related to the problem as requested by the Consultant.

5. Assumptions:

   ▪ Company staff will be available for interviews and review discussion on a timely basis—within a week of request.

   ▪ The Company will provide the Consultant with all documentation related to the project.

6.  Scope Management:

    - Company—If the scope is changed or hypotheses are not agreed to, the cost and timeline will have to be adjusted accordingly.

    - Consultant—If the hypotheses are not proven to be the "right" hypotheses, then another set will be chosen and agreed to by the Company.

7.  Notice of Execution:

    - The implementation of the recommendations made by the Consultant can take many different interpretations; therefore, the Consultant cannot be held responsible for its outcome.

8.  Place Where Services Will Be Rendered:

    - The Consultant will perform most services under this contract at the Company's offices, during virtual sessions, and/or at the Consultant's office.

9.  Staffing and Timeline:

    - The Consultant staffing will consist of a team of four (4) consultants (see bios).

    - The service will be completed in six (6) weeks, beginning when the Agreement is signed and ending six (6) weeks from that date.

10. Billing and Fees:

    - The fees for the consulting services stated in paragraph (1) are $100,000. Consultants will be paid one-half the amount on signing the LOA, and the remainder on completion of the work performed no later than 30 days from the date of the invoice.

## General Provisions

Our work for companies is conducted on a confidential basis. Accordingly, we will preserve the confidential nature of any appropriately designated proprietary information received from you or developed during our work for you.

Either party may use the name of the other for advertising or promotional purposes with prior permission. It is understood that work products resulting from this assignment are intended for your internal use and are not to be used in whole or in part outside your organization. External use of our work products will require our prior written approval. All work products approved for external use will contain a notice that describes the limits and the conditions under which the work products can be distributed and/or used.

Our work will be performed on a best-effort basis consistent with that degree of skill and care customarily exercised by consulting firms performing services of a similar nature. Our total liability arising out of or in connection with the results of our work or any recommendations made according to this Agreement shall not exceed the total compensation paid to us. As a result of this, you agree to release, indemnify, and hold us harmless from and against any costs or liability in excess (including claims against us by third parties). We shall not be liable for any indirect, consequential, special, or incidental losses or damages.

This Agreement (including resolution of any disputes arising hereunder) will be governed by and interpreted according to the laws of the State of Texas.

Signatures: Both the Company and the Consultant agree to the above contract.

| Consultant: | Company: HT Fitness, Inc. |
|---|---|
| Signature: | Signature: |
| Date: | Date: |
| Name: | Name: |
| Title: | Title: |

## CHAPTER SUMMARY

In this chapter, we used all the information that we had collected through meetings and discussions with the client, including information about the client, their issues and problems, and the kind of service they wanted. We developed a well-defined and precise problem statement that frames the consulting engagement and is used to create the contractual agreement with the client.

We detailed the client, consultant, and services, including the timing, terms, and cost. This information was documented in a Letter of Agreement (LOA). We obtained the client's approval to proceed with the consulting engagement based on their authorization (signing of the LOA).

## QUICK QUIZ

Identify at least five major sections of an LOA.

## QUICK QUIZ ANSWERS

Major sections of an LOA are the problem statement, approach and deliverables, scope of services, company responsibilities, assumptions, staffing and timeline, billing and fees, and general provisions.

## DISCUSSION QUESTIONS

1. What is the primary purpose of the LOA?

2. Do you think an LOA will help a client understand what they want to be solved?

## KEY TERMS

**General provisions:** A series of statements defining confidentiality, use of materials, best efforts, and under which state the agreement will be governed by.

**Letter of agreement (LOA):** The contractual agreement between the consultant and client to provide the consulting services specified.

## END NOTES

A letter of Agreement sets out the terms of a working relationship by including information such as the contact information of both parties, the agreed-upon terms, including payment, when the agreement goes into effect, and when it will end.

This type of contract documents a legal agreement between two parties. In contrast, oral contracts are sometimes enforceable, but creating a "Letter of Agreement" strengthens the contract's legality in question. A "Letter of Agreement" is the same as a valid contract.

## REFERENCES

Shenson, Howard L. *Complete Guide to Consulting Success*. Wilmington, DE: Enterprise Publishing, 1991.

Upcounsel. What Is a Letter of Agreement: Everything You Need To Know, 2022. https://www.upcounsel.com/what-is-a-letter-of-agreement

## CREDIT

**CHAPTER 8**

# Manage a Consulting Project

## Introduction

This chapter deals with the topic of a consulting project. You may not realize it but, you have been creating and managing projects your whole life. Humanity has been creating and managing projects for the entire time of human existence. Consulting projects have some commonalities with the projects that you have worked on. However, consultant projects contain elements that will be new to you. In this chapter, we will review project management in general and then discuss different types of ways to manage consulting projects.

## Consulting Project Management

So what is a project? (See Figure 8.1.) The key thing to recognize about a **project** is its definite beginning and end. It also aims to develop a unique service for a client. The goal of providing a service makes consulting different from other projects, such as the building of the pyramids, the creation of the Great Wall of China, and the Apollo moon project. Remember, when you're working on a consulting project that the people around you are working to keep the client business going. We refer to this as **operations**. A key point for a consultant to remember is to work within the client organization. By doing this, the consultant builds goodwill for the changes to come with a successful consulting project. Realize also consulting projects will end at some point in time. That is the nature of projects!

- A **project** is "a temporary endeavor undertaken to create a unique product, service, or result."
- **Operations** is work done to sustain the business.
- A **consulting project** ends when its objectives have been reached or the project has been terminated. It can be large or small and take a short or long time to complete.

FIGURE 8.1  What is a project?

FIGURE 8.2  The triple constraint of project management (the iron triangle)

The **triple constraint** (see Figure 8.2) is a fundamental principle of consultant project management. Sometimes referred to as the iron triangle, the triple constraint sets boundaries on what can be accomplished (scope), how long it will take to complete something (time), and how much it will cost to get it done (cost).

All three are interrelated. Cost is a function of scope and time. Time is a function of cost and scope. And scope is a function of time and cost. What that means is that if you change one of these variables, the other variables have to be changed. For example, if you increase the project scope, you'll have to increase the time and the cost the same. This iron triangle is always in the back of the consultant's mind. Clients frequently will try to increase the scope, and as a consultant, you will need to remind them that this will increase the cost or the time.

To manage a consulting project, the consultant develops steps to complete the project. The different steps to do this are referred to as a **methodology**. Methodologies (see Figure 8.3) refer to a high-level plan (strategic). Methodologies are not overly concerned with the local solution to a particular consulting problem. Methodologies are concerned with how those solutions are developed and implemented. Methodologies are concerned with grouping appropriate actions into phases and what these phases produce. The output of the phases are the deliverables. Methodologies are also concerned with what tools are used to manage a consulting project. For example, what reports are required, how frequently are the reports required, and in what format (electronic or paper), and the content of the reports.

Finally, methodologies refer to the idea of knowledge areas. Knowledge areas require particular sets of knowledge the consultant will need to solve the business problem they are working on. For example, a consultant who is working on an accounting problem will need to be knowledgeable about accounting. Always, the consultant must consider how to be flexible in solving the business problem.

A **strategic-level plan** for managing and controlling consulting projects does the following:

- Recommends phases, deliverables, processes, tools, and knowledge areas; and
- Is flexible and includes best practices learned from experience over time.

FIGURE 8.3  Methodology

Inevitably, change will occur. A successful consultant can adapt to change and continue to solve the business problem.

A methodology will group all the pieces from beginning to end. The grouping is called a **project life cycle**. It connects all the phases, deliverables, processes, tools, and knowledge areas (see Figure 8.4).

There is a distinct life cycle for a consulting project. Figure 8.5 shows the five distinct phases of the consulting life cycle. These phases are discussed in greater detail in other chapters in this text. Combining the various phases in a particular order is a methodology.

> A **project life cycle** is a collection of project phases that define the following:
>
> - What work will be performed in each phase;
> - What deliverables will be produced and when;
> - Who will be involved in each phase; and
> - How management will control and approve work produced ineach phase.

FIGURE 8.4  Project phases and the project life cycle

The **consulting project life cycle** consists of five phases. Each phase has a purpose, related processes, and deliverables associated with it.

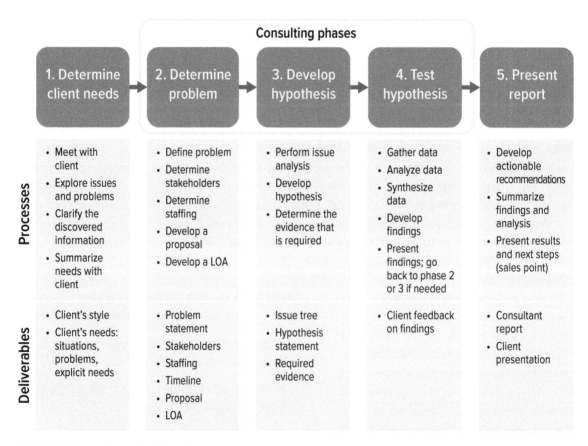

| | Consulting phases | | | |
|---|---|---|---|---|
| **1. Determine client needs** | **2. Determine problem** | **3. Develop hypothesis** | **4. Test hypothesis** | **5. Present report** |
| **Processes** | | | | |
| • Meet with client<br>• Explore issues and problems<br>• Clarify the discovered information<br>• Summarize needs with client | • Define problem<br>• Determine stakeholders<br>• Determine staffing<br>• Develop a proposal<br>• Develop a LOA | • Perform issue analysis<br>• Develop hypothesis<br>• Determine the evidence that is required | • Gather data<br>• Analyze data<br>• Synthesize data<br>• Develop findings<br>• Present findings; go back to phase 2 or 3 if needed | • Develop actionable recommendations<br>• Summarize findings and analysis<br>• Present results and next steps (sales point) |
| **Deliverables** | | | | |
| • Client's style<br>• Client's needs: situations, problems, explicit needs | • Problem statement<br>• Stakeholders<br>• Staffing<br>• Timeline<br>• Proposal<br>• LOA | • Issue tree<br>• Hypothesis statement<br>• Required evidence | • Client feedback on findings | • Consultant report<br>• Client presentation |

FIGURE 8.5  Consulting project life cycle

### Phase 1: Develop Client Needs

The purpose is to build a relationship with the client and determine their need(s). Chapter 3 discusses determining the client's style and forming a rapport and good communication to build a trusting relationship. This enables you to explore their issues and problems and leads to determining their explicit need(s) (see Chapter 4).

### Phase 2: Determine the Problem

The purpose of this phase is to refine the client's explicit need into a precise problem statement (see Chapter 6) that frames and focuses the engagement. The problem statement defines the scope and domain of what the client wants to be answered. During this phase, we also identify the stakeholder (see Chapter 5) and their role in the engagement. Finally, the scope, domain, and stakeholders give the consultant the needed information to create a proposal and Letter of Agreement (see Chapter 7) to begin the engagement (i.e., project).

### Phase 3: Develop the Hypothesis

This phase aims to determine possible answers to the client's problem by performing an analysis (e.g., issue analysis) and defining several hypotheses and evidence required to prove or disprove (see Chapter 9).

### Phase 4: Test Hypothesis

This phase aims to gather evidence (data) and analyze it to determine if the hypothesis is true or false (see Chapter 10). The findings are presented to the client and may require the consultant to refine the problem statement (phase 2) or refine the hypothesis (phase 3). Looping back and giving feedback to the client each time helps everyone to understand the problem and provides a clearer answer and sets the basis for making recommendations.

### Phase 5: Present the Report

This phase looks to develop actionable recommendations from the findings (see Chapter 11) that will enable the client to solve their problem(s) and move their organization forward. The results are documented in a presentable report to the client, including the next steps.

    The deliverables and processes for each phase are defined in the chapters referenced above. Consulting projects require continuous communication with the client throughout the project. Communication is key to the client's acceptance of the consultant's recommendations.

## Waterfall Project Management Methodology

Two methodologies are used in managing projects that build things. The first is the **Waterfall method**, and the second is the **Agile method**.

    Engineers first developed the Waterfall project management methodology to construct bridges, buildings, dams, and other structures. The engineers who developed the Waterfall project management methodology knew the requirements of the product they were building before they started. Therefore, no change of requirements takes place during the project. For example, imagine a bridge that was halfway through the project and the bridge dimensions were changed. It would be complete chaos, and the bridge project would not succeed.

The Waterfall project management life cycle has many of the same phases as the consulting project life cycle. For example, requirements gathering and understanding the problem are common to the consulting project life cycle and the Waterfall project life cycle (Figure 8.6). The Waterfall project management methodology applied to the consulting life cycle has many shortcomings—very limited involvement of the client, for example, and evolving requirements from the client. All of this led to the development of other project methodologies. Most notably is the development of the Agile project methodology.

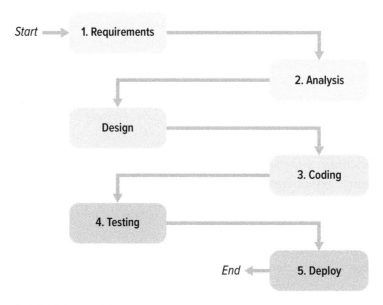

FIGURE 8.6 Waterfall project management methodology

## Agile Project Management Methodology

Over the last 25 years, the new project management methodology has evolved. It is referred to as Agile project management methodology (see Figure 8.7). This project methodology, was developed originally for developing information technology software and hardware, is being used increasingly in consulting. Agile project management methodology has the following characteristics:

- Iterative and incremental approach
- Cross-functional teams
- Short iterations
- Highest value item first
- Continuous feedback and improvement
- Streamlined and time-boxed
- Business priorities and customer values

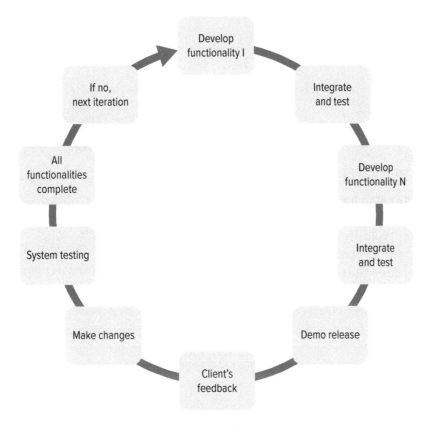

FIGURE 8.7  Agile project management methodology

## Agile Project Management Methodology Iterative and Incremental

Agile project management methodology proceeds in an interactive manner. This means that as the project continues, there are cycles that are completed. Each cycle builds upon the previous cycle, not only on what is created but what is learned in the previous cycle. There is no limit to the number of iterations.

FIGURE 8.8  Agile project management methodology iterative and incremental

## Agile Project Management Methodology: Cross-functional Teams

As the name implies, in Agile project methodology, **cross-functional teams** are composed of selected members from the consulting team (Dev Team) and subject matter expert's (SME) for a particular iteration. This permits the team to focus on the iteration.

Agile project management methodology has the following characteristics:

- Short iterations

- Highest value item first

- Continuous feedback and improvement

- Streamlined and time-boxed

- Business priorities and customer values

Agile iterations typically range from two to three weeks. During that period, the consulting team produces the most important deliverable for the client. This permits

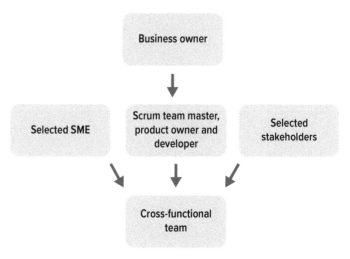

FIGURE 8.9 Adapted from Agile project management methodology cross-functional teams

the client to provide continuous feedback to the consulting team and the consulting team to improve on the deliverable. Limiting time for each iteration permits the consulting team to focus on a particular deliverable. Ultimately, this permits the consulting team to focus on the customer's business priorities and values.

## Agile Project Management Values

The Agile project management methodology has primary values. Comparing the Agile primary values to the secondary values coming from the Waterfall project management. Figure 8.10 shows the comparison of these primary and secondary values. These primary values are summarized as focused on customer needs, respect for individuals, and adapting to the change in business environment. These values and Agile principles are shown in Figures 8.10 and 8.11.

**Primary values**
- Individuals and interactions
- Working product
- Customer collaboration
- Responding to change

**Secondary values**
- Processes and tools
- Comprehensive documentation
- Contract negotiation
- Following a plan

FIGURE 8.10 Agile project management methodology—values

- Satisfy the customer
- Welcome change
- Deliver frequently
- Work together
- Motivate individuals
- Use face-to-face communication
- Working product
- Constant pace
- Technical excellence
- Simplicity
- Self-organizing teams
- Reflection

FIGURE 8.11 Agile project management methodology—principles

## Comparing the Two Consulting Project Methodologies

The choice of project methodologies to use is up to the consulting team. It is useful to compare the two methodologies. The consulting company, the Standish Group, has followed the success of project management methodologies since the 1980s. The Standish Group originally did this in response to the failures of

| Method | Successful | Challenged | Failed |
|--------|-----------|------------|--------|
| Agile | 42% | 47% | 11% |
| Waterfall | 13% | 59% | 28% |

FIGURE 8.12  Project success rates Agile versus Waterfall

IT projects. Over the years, the Standish Group has seen the traditional Waterfall method evolve. In particular, the Standish Group has been tracking the rise of Agile project management methodology since 2000.

The most recent study published in 2020 compared traditional Waterfall project management methodologies to Agile project methodologies. The results are striking and are summarized in Figure 8.12. The comparison shows that the Agile project management methodology is four times as successful as the traditional Waterfall methodology. The comparison also shows that Agile project management methodology is three times less likely to fail than the traditional Waterfall methodology.

## Project Plans

Organize your projects with project plans to keep things on track before you even start. A project plan contains all the necessary details of your project, such as goals, tasks, scope, deadlines, communications, and deliverables. The plan shows stakeholders a clear roadmap of your project, ensures you have the resources for it, and holds everyone accountable from the start. Project plans are sometimes called work plans.

A project charter is an outline of a project plan—it should only include your project objectives, scope (size and boundaries), and responsibilities.

Project plans set the stage for the entire project. Without one, you're missing the first critical step in the overall project management process. Launching a project without defined goals or objectives can lead to disorganized work, frustration, and even scope creep. A clear, written project management plan provides a baseline direction to all stakeholders while keeping everyone accountable. In addition, it confirms that you have the resources you need for the project before it begins.

A project plan also allows the consultant in charge of leading execution to forecast potential challenges while the project is still in the planning stages. That way, the consultant can ensure the project will be achievable—or course-correct if necessary.

According to a study conducted by the Project Management Institute, there is a strong correlation between project planning and project success—the better your plan, the better your outcome. So, conquering the planning phase also improves project efficiency and results.

A clear project management plan provides a way to track all of the moving parts during the execution of the projects and includes:

- Goals and project objectives

- Success metrics

- Stakeholders and roles

- Scope and budget

- Communication plan

- Issue management

- Milestones, deliverables, and project dependencies

- Task schedule with assignments and due dates

There are several steps to completing the project plan.

## Step 1: Define the Goals and Objectives

Every successful project plan should have a clear desired outcome. Identifying your goals provides a rationale for your project plan. It also keeps everyone on the same page and focused on the results they want to achieve. The project goals should be at a higher level than your project objectives. The project goals should be "SMART goals" that help you measure project success and show how your project aligns with the client's business. SMART is an acronym to help you create defined and attainable goals. SMART stands for **S**pecific, **M**easurable, **A**chievable, **R**ealistic, and **T**ime-bound.

Your project plan provides the direction your team needs to hit your goals through the project objectives. The purpose of drafting project objectives is to focus on the actual, specific deliverables created by the end of your project.

## Step 2: Set Success Metrics

Once goals are defined, make sure they're measurable by setting key success metrics. While a goal serves as the intended result, develop success metrics to determine whether or not the project is performing on track to achieve that result. The best way to do that is to set SMART goals as defined previously. SMART goals make sure your success metrics are clear and measurable.

## Step 3: Clarify Stakeholders and Roles

Running a project usually means getting collaborators involved in the execution. In your project management plan, outline which team members will be a part of the project and each person's role. This will help you decide who is responsible for each task and lets stakeholders know how you expect them to be involved.

During this process, define the various roles and responsibilities your stakeholders might have. For example, who is directly responsible for the project's success? Are there any approvers that should be involved before anything is finalized? What cross-functional stakeholders should be included in the project plan? Are there any risk management factors that need to be included? Then, after outlining your roles and stakeholders, ensure that documentation is included in your project plan.

## Step 4: Set Your Budget

Since goals and stakeholders have been defined as part of your project plan, use that information to establish your budget. By setting your project budget during the project planning phase (and before the spending begins), you can get approval, more easily track progress, and make wise, economic decisions during the implementation phase of your project. Knowing your budget beforehand helps with resource management, ensuring that the project stays within the initial financial scope of the project. In addition, planning helps determine what parts of your project will cost—leaving no room for later surprises.

## Step 5: Align Milestones, Deliverables, and Project Dependencies

An essential part of planning your project is setting milestones or specific objectives representing an achievement. Milestones don't require a start and end date, but hitting one marks a significant accomplishment during your project. They are used to measure progress. For example, let's say the project is to develop a new website for the client. Setting a milestone on your project timeline for when the website framework is finalized will help measure the progress.

A project deliverable, on the other hand, is what is produced once you meet a milestone. When a milestone is hit, a deliverable is produced. You can also use project dependencies—tasks can't start until others are finished. Dependencies ensure that work only starts once it's ready.

## Step 6: Outline Your Timeline and Schedule

In order to achieve your project goals, you and your stakeholders need clarity on your overall project timeline and schedule. Once the high-level responsibilities are covered, it's time to focus some energy on the details. Start by breaking your project into tasks, ensuring no part of the process is skipped. More significant tasks can be broken down into smaller subtasks, making them more manageable. Guidelines for tasks include:

- One person per task (clear responsibility)

- Binary results; either completed or not (need new forecast)

- Clear start and end; completion can be observed (i.e., deliverable or section of)

- Duration should be 3 to 5 days (if 20% off, only one day to catch up)

- Minimum interaction between tasks (tightly bound and deliverable coupled)

- Reviewed weekly

## Step 7: Share Your Communication Plan

Most projects include multiple stakeholders. That means communication styles will vary among them. Set your expectations up front for the project. A communication plan is essential for ensuring everyone understands what's happening, how the project is progressing, and what's going on next. And if a roadblock comes up, a clear communication system will be in place. Items to include in the communication plan include:

- Regular meeting dates and times; include how: in-person (where); virtual (what platform)
- Weekly status reports; who should they go to and where are they stored (e.g., project wiki; see Chapter 14)
- Issue list; assigned responsibility, due dates, and who should review it weekly
- Assign a project team member for each part of the communication plan

| Description | Frequency | Channel | Audience | Owner |
|---|---|---|---|---|
| Project status updates | Weekly | MS Teams | All internal stakeholders and project team members | Project manager |
| Project team meetings | Bi-weekly | Zoom | All project team members, stakeholders optional | Project manager |
| External stakeholders updates | As needed | Zoom | Project manager and project stakeholders | Project sponsor |
| Milestones and deliverables updates | As needed | MS Teams | Project team | All project team members |
| Project check-ins | Daily | MS Teams | Project team | All project team members |

FIGURE 8.13  Communication plan

## CHAPTER SUMMARY

This chapter introduced the concept of project methodology as it can be used in consulting. Consulting project management has unique needs and uses a particular set of phases:

1. Determine client needs
2. Determine problem
3. Develop hypothesis
4. Test hypothesis
5. Present recommendations

Waterfall project management methodology is the traditional project methodology used for consulting projects. Waterfall project management methodology is characterized as 1) defined and linear; and 2) highly structured. Agile project management methodology is a new project methodology used for consulting projects. Agile project management methodology has the following characteristics:

- Iterative and incremental approach
- Cross-functional teams
- Short iterations
- Highest value item first
- Continuous feedback and improvement
- Streamlined and time-boxed
- Business priorities and customer values

Agile project management values focus on 1) individuals and interactions; 2) working product; 3) customer collaboration; and 4) responding to change. Comparing the two consulting project methodologies, Agile project management is four times as likely to succeed as Waterfall project management methodology.

## QUICK QUIZ

1. The Agile way is which of the following?

   a. To produce a working product early and incrementally

   b. To produce working product after documentation has been signed off

   c. To produce simple prototypes early, but no finished product until the end of the project

   d. To produce products without any technical integrity

2. All the following are Agile values except which of the following?

   a. Working Product over Comprehensive Documentation

   b. Customer Collaboration over Contract Negotiation

   c. Gated Delivery over Iterative Development

   d. Individuals and Interactions over Processes and Tools

3. What is deliverable for the hypothesis phase of consulting project management?

   a. Identifying key stakeholders

   b. Completing a business case

   c. Assigning the project manager

   d. Issue tree

## QUICK QUIZ ANSWERS

1. The Agile way is: a. To produce a working product early and incrementally.

2. All the following are Agile values except: c. Gated Delivery over Iterative Development.

3. What is deliverable for the hypothesis phase of consulting project management? d. Issue tree

## DISCUSSION QUESTIONS

1. Briefly discuss the five phases of the consulting project.

2. Compare and contrast Waterfall project management methodology and Agile project management methodology.

3. Describe a project methodology.

## KEY TERMS

**Project:** An engagement of a client and a consultant that has a beginning and an ending and produces a service or product for the client.

**Operations:** Work performed to sustain a business.

**Triple constraint:** A set of constraints that sets boundaries of Scope, Cost, and Time.

**Methodology:** A set of processes and deliverables produced during the execution of a project with the use of tools.

**Project life cycle:** A collection of project phases that defines what, when and how deliverables will be produced in the execution of a project, including who/role is involved. It is also involved with the management of each phase.

**Hypothesis:** An assumption, an idea proposed for the sake of argument so that it can be tested to see if it might be true.

**Waterfall model:** A sequential development process that flows like a waterfall through all phases of a project (analysis, design, development, and testing, for example), with each phase completely wrapping up before the next phase begins.

**Agile model:** An iterative approach to project management and software development that helps teams deliver value to their customers faster and with fewer headaches

**Iterative development:** A way of breaking down the software development of a large application into smaller chunks, that are designed, developed and tested in repeated cycles.

**Cross-functional teams:** Groups consisting of people from different functional areas of the company—for example, marketing, product, sales, and customer success.

**Time-boxed:** A defined period of time during which a task must be accomplished.

## REFERENCES

Baca, Claudia. *Project Manager's Spotlight on Change Management.* San Francisco: Harbour Light Press, 2005.

Beck, Kent. *Extreme Programming Explained: Embrace Change.* Indianapolis: Pearson, 2001.

Manas, Jerry. *Napoleon on Project Management: Timeless Lessons in Planning Execution and Leadership.* Nashville: Thomas Nelson, 2006.

Shenhar, Aaron, and Dov Dvir. *Reinventing Project Management: The Diamond Approach to Successful Growth and Innovation.* Boston: Harvard Business School, 2007.

Thomsett, Rob. *Radical Project Management.* Upper saddle River, NJ: Prentice Hall, 2002.

Williams, Todd C. *Rescue the Problem Project: A Complete Guide to Identifying, Recovering, and Presenting Project Failure.* New York: American Management Association, 2011.

## CREDITS

## CHAPTER 9

# Developing the Hypothesis

**LEARNING OBJECTIVES**

After reading this chapter, students will be able to:

- Determine an answer to the client's question (problem statement).
- Create a detailed issue analysis tree of the case study of HT Fitness that is in Chapter 14.9.
- Create a hypothesis for each sub-issue in the issue tree for the HT Fitness case.

## Introduction

Why is the development of a hypothesis important to a consulting project? It is actually part of the secret sauce of management consulting. It's more than educated guessing; this is how consultants smartly break down complex or ambiguous problems and quickly start driving toward an answer. At its heart is the scientific method—used for centuries by scientists and thinkers to prove their ideas using **evidence**.

Why is it difficult to frame the problem issue? Generally, the key question (i.e., the problem to be solved) on what the engagement is built on is not well defined or formed in the client's mind. This is why we go through the detailed process of determining the client's needs (as seen in Chapter 3) and refining what we find (Chapter 6) by defining the problem that the client wants to be solved. Typically, there are many things that the client sees as making the problem complex, as depicted in Figure 9.1. These include the following:

- Critical unknowns
- Multiple stakeholders and departments are affected
- Not enough data is available
- The time and resources needed are problematic
- Lack of skill sets necessary
- Ill-defined

The primary purpose of consulting is to provide expert advice to solve the client's problem. The engagement is conducted in phases, with **hypothesis** development at its heart. The phases are shown in Figure 9.2. Notice there is a recycling loop between defining the problem and testing the hypothesis. During testing of the hypothesis, the chosen hypothesis may not be proven true, and the consultant has to go back to previous phases and determine a better set of hypotheses.

The problem analysis (hypothesis development) is accomplished using many proven tools by successful consulting firms: McKinsey & Company, Booz Allen Hamilton, Bain & Company, Boston Consulting Group, Accenture, and PricewaterhouseCoopers (PWC). However, some tools are thought to be better suited to this analysis process than others and are used more frequently.

FIGURE 9.1  Client problem illustration

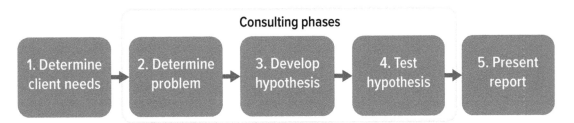

FIGURE 9.2  Consulting phases

Some of the tools for structuring the problem to arrive at a solution include the following:

- SWOT Analysis
- Porter's 5 Forces
- Profit Analysis
- Multiple-Criteria Decision Analysis
- Issue Analysis

## SWOT Analysis

SWOT analysis is a straightforward framework that can be thought of as a background analysis method that is second nature to most and allows for a big-picture view.

- **S**trengths: Internal characteristics of the client's business that give it an advantage over others

- **W**eaknesses: Internal characteristics of the client's business that give it a disadvantage compared to others

- **O**pportunities: External elements that the client's business could use to its advantage

- **T**hreats: External elements in the environment that could cause trouble for the client's business

A SWOT analysis should give a client confidence and a better idea of what strategic direction to go in and what issues or problems should be dealt with.

## Porter's Five Forces

Porter's five forces are a framework for analyzing a company's competitive position. The number and capabilities of a company's competitive rivals, threats of new market entrants, suppliers' bargaining power, customers' bargaining power, and the threat of substitute products influence the company's profitability. This is essential for understanding the forces that constitute competition in an industry. In addition, it helps develop a company's strategy based on the environment.

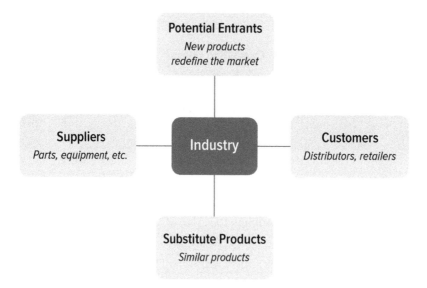

FIGURE 9.3  Porter's five forces

## Profit Analysis

Profit analysis involves breaking down the profit figure of a business to determine the actual level of its profitability. Outside analysts commonly utilize this analysis due to the often inflated profit information presented to people outside the company. Typically, these ratios are used in this analysis. The most common are net profit margin, operating profit margin, and EBITDA margin.

## Multiple-Criteria Decision Analysis (MCDA)

Multiple-criteria decision analysis is a decision-making analysis that evaluates multiple (conflicting) criteria as part of the decision-making process. It allows the consultant to rank alternatives based on an evaluation according to several criteria. Then, decisions are made based on trade-offs or compromises among several conflicting criteria. It is a good tool for selecting hardware or software solutions. See Chapter 14.5 for details on conducting the MCDA method.

## Issue Analysis (Pyramid Principle)

This analysis methodology is a particular way of solving problems for clients. This framework is not necessarily the best 100% of the time, but it is the best framework for 85% of business consulting issues.

Issue analysis is implicit in Barbara Minto's recommended writing style (see Chapter 14.6 for details). Issues are grouped in "pyramids." Minto codified rules for pyramids. Actual practice results in the application of the rules.

## What Is Issue Analysis?

It's the application of a structured logic process to solve business problems. The process is very results oriented and has three components:

- Problem definition

- Task delineation

- Client communications

It's a process to answer a client's key question, develop a problem definition, or resolve a key issue by using the following (**SCQA**):

- Situation: What is the issue or problem?

- Complication: What's wrong?

- Question: Depending on the complication, here's the question

- Answer: Here's what should be done

## Structure and Framework

A pyramidal structure is utilized. Each idea must be logical and the same type and level of information within each level of the pyramid. Every level higher in the pyramid summarizes results from the level below it. The information is communicated in the same SCQ outlined in Chapter 6.

What the answer is can trigger decisions or recommendations of action. Typically, the high-level question (issue) is identified and broken into lower-level sub-issues that can make the problem more manageable. Identifying issues means finding the right questions.

- Creates a hierarchy of questions

- Develops a logical structure within the questions

- Implies work tasks to answer the questions

## What Is an Issue?

There is no reliable definition of what constitutes an issue. Issues are questions with a "Yes" or "No" answer and are relevant. They suggest a path of analysis and provide a framework for management action. Client problems are statements of situations where management is uncertain about what to do, and there is typically a question.

# Issue Analysis for Hypotheses Development

## How Does It Relate to Hypotheses Development?

Issues relate to the hypothesis because they are significant pieces of the problem. They are limited in scope, size, and number. They are phrased as questions and are amenable to being closed out. Hypotheses support either proving or disproving the issues. The relationship is outlined below:

TABLE 9.1  **Issue Versus Hypothesis**

| Issue? | Hypothesis? |
|---|---|
| Major piece of the problem | Posed as a statement to be proved or disproved |
| Supports client concerns | A "hunch" or educated guess |
| Limited in number | Falls under an issue |
| Posed as a question | Gives a tentative answer |
| Able to be closed | Provides direction for information gathering |

## Creating an Issue Analysis

The key to using issue analysis is to define the problem that the client wants to solve. Determining the key question drives the development of the issues and hypotheses needed to develop a solution.

Developing the key question is about determining where the client is currently and where the client wants to be. The strategic question is how to close the gap between those two states.

Once you have determined the key strategic question, you move to issue analysis development. Issues need to have a Yes or No answer. The key question will be defined by the situation and the cause of uncertainty (see Chapter 6). Develop sub-questions to drive the answer to the key issue and make the problem more manageable. These sub-questions/issues put boundaries on what is to be addressed in the engagement. List enough issues/sub-issues to answer the key question. This helps avoid unimportant questions and analyses to "boil the ocean."

## Process of Developing a Tree

The basic steps in the issues analysis process build on one another.

1. Define the key question in the client's mind.

2. Break the overall question into issues to make the problem more manageable and granular. Issues should be answers to the "how" or "why." The issues defined must follow **MECE** (**m**utually **e**xclusive and **c**ollectively **e**xhaustive, see Chapter 14.5) to ensure that some area is not missing.

3. Develop sub-issue questions which are answerable with a "Yes" or "No."

4. Create a hierarchy of questions that develop a logical structure, implying work tasks to answer the questions.

5. Be familiar with inductive versus deductive reasoning as it applies to how you structure issue answers.

    a. Induction defines a group of facts or ideas as the same thing and then makes a statement (or inference) about the sameness image 9.1.

    b. Deduction presents a line of reasoning that leads to a "therefore" conclusion, and the point above summarizes that line of reasoning, resting heavily on the final point image 9.2.

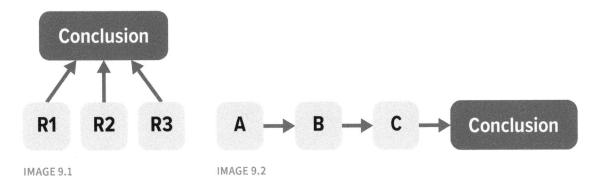

IMAGE 9.1                IMAGE 9.2

6. Remember, structured logic's rules for structuring a "point" in an argument apply to issue structures.

    a. Points must address the question or problem directly

    b. Points must raise a question

    c. The key line must answer the question

    **d.** Key line "points" must

       **i.** follow rules

      **ii.** be logical

    **iii.** be important

    **e.** Be relevant. The issue breakdown depends on the situation.

## Summary: Problems of Putting Issue Analysis into Practice

The consultant who does not take the time necessary to adequately get agreement with the client on the key issue troubling the company hinders putting issue analysis into practice.

Another problem for the consultant is moving forward with a preconceived notion of the solution to the client's problem without working through the process of defining the issues, developing the hypothesis, testing the hypothesis, modifying the hypothesis; and developing the answers that provide the client's resolution and an action path forward.

The best answer is derived from the work effort involved in the issue analysis and data gathered to prove or disprove the issues identified. The issue analysis process allows the consultant to break down a complex problem into a well-defined flow of issues, sub-issues, and tasks to prove or disprove the hypotheses. For example, see the relationships of the components in Figure 9.4.

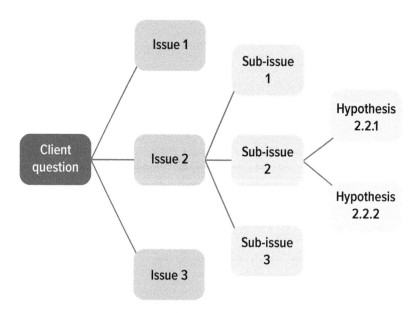

FIGURE 9.4  Relationship of issues to hypothesis

## Example of Issue Analysis for the Reference Case HT Fitness (Found in Chapter 14.9)

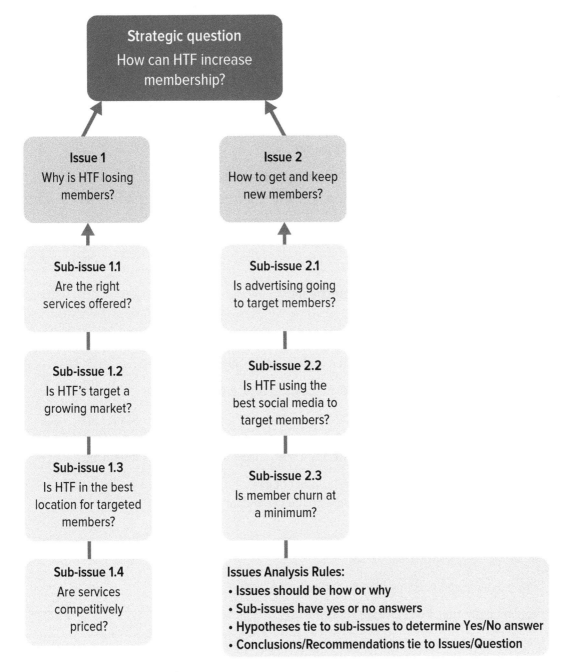

FIGURE 9.5 HT Fitness issue analysis tree

# Hypothesis Development

## What Is a Business Hypothesis?

A hypothesis is a testable statement about the relationship between two or more variables or a proposed explanation for some observed phenomenon. It can include the initial assumptions, or it may be a theory that is yet tested. A hypothesis is therefore not always true. Instead, it is a starting point that ultimately leads you to the endpoint. For example, a business hypothesis is an assumption that your value proposition, business model, or strategy builds on to succeed.

A reasonable hypothesis must possess the following characteristics:

- It is never formulated in the form of a question.

- It should be empirically testable, whether it is right or wrong.

- It should be specific and precise.

- It should specify variables between which the relationship is to be established.

## Essential Elements of Building a Hypothesis

- Define the problem/question you are trying to solve.

- Ensure the hypothesis clearly defines the problem to be solved.

- Develop a hypothesis as an IF ... THEN statement, if possible.

- Define the variables.

Since a hypothesis is an educated guess, it is often written as an IF and THEN statement.

> IF I don't put gas in the car, THEN I will run out of gas
> This form (IF ... THEN) reflects independent and dependent variables.

## Examples of If ... Then Form

- If I buy premium gas, then my car will get better mileage.

- If I eat less daily, then I will lose weight faster.

- If I replace my car's battery, my car will get better gas mileage.

- If I eat more vegetables, then I will lose weight faster.

- If I add fertilizer to my garden, then my plants will grow faster.

- If I brush my teeth every day, then I will not develop cavities.

## Other Examples of Not in If ... Then Form

- Market consolidates around three major platforms—iOS, Android, and Win 8.

- Users will shift content consumption (and hence ads) away from PCs to tablets.

- The current trend of a shift in advertising dollars will accelerate, and online advertising will increase dramatically.

- Rich media advertising supported by open standards on both apps and browsers likely to accelerate.

- Five major ways to play in the display ad market: integrator, aggregator, distributor, platform enabler, and premium/niche.

## Developing a Good Hypothesis

- Connect the dots based on general and specific experience and research.

- Do the homework—literature searches, web searches, books, journals.

- Engage with different groups of people—planning and brainstorming meetings (see Chapter 14.2), client meeting getting their insight, colleagues.

- Stand on the shoulders of others—experts in a particular field, practice guides, and other similar assignments.

- Gather preliminary data—industry analysis, product/service reviews, census data, etc.

- Do critical thinking  and brainstorm with colleagues.

# Example of Hypotheses and Rationale from the Case

## Let's Review the Problem-Solving Process

We developed the **issue tree** (key issues, sub-issues). Next, we built a hypothesis for each sub-issue. Then, we found evidence to prove or disprove the hypothesis. Then, we tested the evidence collected to determine if it proved or disproved the hypothesis. We keep the client informed of the results of the process steps throughout the engagement. Finally, we document our findings and recommendations and present them to the client as shown in Figure 9.6.

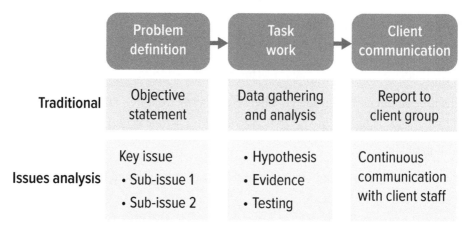

FIGURE 9.6  Problem-solving process

## HT Fitness Case Examples

Based on the HT Fitness case (as shown in Figure 9.5), let's look at a few sub-issues and related hypotheses and the rationale.

- Sub-Issue 1.1. Are the right services offered?

- Hypothesis 1. If yoga classes are offered, then more women would join HT Fitness.

The rationale is that HT Fitness currently has a low volume of women members and would like to add more. The evidence would be found by testing if women would join if HT Fitness offered yoga classes. Accomplish through interviews, targeted questionnaires, etc. You may have to go through a list of all current and future services to determine.

- Sub-Issue 1.4. Are services competitively priced?

- Hypothesis 2. Our prices are assumed to align with our competition.

The rationale is that management believes pricing is on par with other facility providers. This assumption needs to be validated against the competition and the offerings from the competition. Evidence to validate would be through market analysis, survey, contacting competitors anonymously, etc.

## Building the Hypothesis

### Treat Hypotheses Like Suspects

Using the analogy of a TV detective, the detectives will not rule out any suspects initially. Instead, they would survey the crime scene and start formulating ideas on who the suspects were, based on eyewitness accounts, clues, and experience. Then, they would keep sleuthing for clues until they were confident that the suspect was either guilty or not guilty.

The same thing is true with the hypothesis. The goal is to put together a list of hypotheses ("suspects," using the crime analogy) that are distinct and separate. Then, start going down the list to figure out if they are guilty or not. Finally, divvy up and conquer the hypothesis list with your consulting team.

## Relationship Between Issue Hypothesis and Evidence

We create the issue and sub-issues by performing an issue analysis tree described earlier in this chapter. The next step is to create one or more hypotheses for each sub-issue. Then, we must determine what evidence is needed to prove or disprove these hypotheses. What is the evidence? Figure 9.7 shows the relations between the different components with examples.

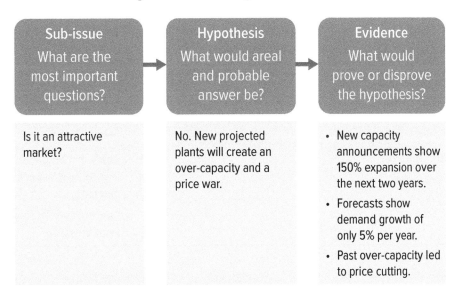

FIGURE 9.7  Issue versus hypothesis versus evidence

Think of the evidence (i.e., data) needed in two dimensions:

- **Method of obtaining the data:** Interview, focus groups, research, surveys, and observations.

- **Source of data:** Client data, client's competition. client's customers, industry sources, government data, e.g., census data (Google Earth has overlays of census data).

Try to find data that can collaborate with the data you first collect. This makes the case stronger that your answer is indeed correct.

Table 9.2 shows several good business examples of laying out the evidence required to make valid data-driven findings and recommendations.

TABLE 9.2  **Issue–Hypothesis–Evidence**

| Issue / (Sub-Issues) | Hypothesis | Evidence Required |
|---|---|---|
| Issue: Good technical decision?<br><br>• Is old machine not meeting quality and quantity? | Yes, for the following reasons:<br><br>• Customer returns are increasing<br>• QA rework is increasing<br>• Back orders are increasing<br>• Daily output declining | • Time series on returns<br>• Time series on rework<br>• Back orders as a percent of sales<br>• Daily production records |
| Issue: Economically sound?<br><br>• Will the machine recover costs? | Yes, for the following reasons:<br><br>• Saving will occur with the new machine<br>• Saving will pay back the cost within four months<br>• The machine will be durable | • Cost accounting projections<br>• Compare monthly savings with the purchase price<br>• Experience of other companies |
| Issue: Do we have money?<br><br>• Do we have the necessary cash?<br>• Is cash uncommitted?<br>• Are attractive terms available? | • Yes, it is in the bank<br>• Yes, cash is surplus<br>• Yes, financing is offered | • Check balance sheet<br>• Collect statement by Finance & Planning V<br>• Confirm manufacturer's captive lease subsidiary covers the machine<br>• Confirm specific loans available from the bank |

## CHAPTER SUMMARY

There are several approaches to determine the answer to the problem statement:

• SWOT analysis

• Porter's five forces

• Profit analysis

• MCDA

• Issue analysis

The issue analysis approach is used to find solutions and recommendations to the client's problem statement in 80 to 90% of business client engagements. The issue analysis approach is discussed using the HT Fitness Organization case (case details can be found in Chapter 14.9).

Many significant business consulting firms like McKinsey, Boston Group, etc., use this approach to handle their cases (client engagements). The basic steps to issue analysis are:

1. Define the overall question (problem statement) the client wants to answer.

2. Determine the significant issues; and they should be about how or why?

3. Break down the issues into sub-issues that have Yes/No answers.

4. Determine one or more hypotheses for each sub-issue.

5. Brainstorm what evidence is required to prove or disprove the hypothesis, answered by Yes or No.

6. Implement tasks to develop/acquire the evidence to prove or disprove the hypothesis.

7. Document the results of finding; make recommendations.

## QUICK QUIZ

1. What are the three primary tools for finding solutions to business problems?

2. Which tool is useful in 85+% of business consulting assignments?

## QUICK QUIZ ANSWERS

1. SWOT analysis, Porter's five forces, profit analysis, MCDA, issue analysis

2. Issue analysis

## DISCUSSION QUESTIONS

1. Why is HT Fitness losing members? Base your discussion on the HT Fitness case data, charts, etc., found in Chapter 14.9.

2. Brainstorm a possible hypothesis for sub-issue 2.2. Is the HT Fitness case using the best social media for target members? Include what the evidence should be.

## KEY TERMS

**Evidence:** The available body of facts or information indicating whether a proposition is true or false (Yes/No)

**Hypothesis:** A proposed explanation made on a basis for reasoning without any assumptions of its truth (Yes/No)

**Issue tree:** A pivotal tool to answer the central question the client is asking by breaking the issue into sub-issues and determining at least one hypothesis for each sub-issue

**MECE: M**utually **E**xclusive and **C**ollectively **E**xhaustive. When we divide data or ideas, have we covered the entire scope of the problem, and are our parts independent?

**SCQ:** Understand the **s**ituation, determine the **c**omplication, formulate the key **q**uestion.

## END NOTES

Additional reading to better understand the key principles of problem solving and providing recommendations to clients.

**Minto Principle.** Consultants must structure their thinking. This is the best way to present your ideas clearly to clients. One excellent tool is the pyramid principle by an ex-McKinsey consultant named Barbara Minto. She authored *The Minto Pyramid Principle*, which essentially defined the way consultants structure most of their presentations. Most consultants will know the pyramid principle, even if they don't know the author.

The **Pyramid Principle** advocates that "ideas should always form a pyramid under a single thought." The single thought is the answer to the key question. Underneath the single thought, you should group and summarize the next level of supporting ideas and arguments.

In a previous chapter, we determined the client's explicit need. The best way to express that need is a problem statement. The best way for the consultant to structure their thinking for developing a problem statement is to use the Minto approach SCQ to:

- Understand the client's **s**ituation

- Determine the **c**omplexities related to the **s**ituation

- Develop the **q**uestion that the client wants to answered

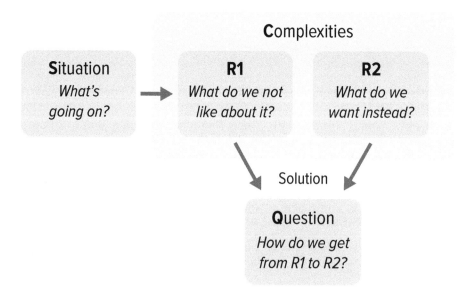

FIGURE 9.8  Adapted from SCQ diagram

## REFERENCES

jkstrategy@consultantsmind.com. *What Is Hypothesis-based Consulting? Consultant's Mind Blog*, 2017. https://www. consultantsmind.com/2017/07/10/hypothesis-based-consulting-2/

Kapoor, Amit. Analytics in Consulting, 2012. https://www.slideshare.net/amitkaps/analytics-in-consulting

Minto, Barbara. *The Pyramid Principle: Logic in Writing and Thinking*. Minto International, 1987.

Superior IS. *Issues Analysis*. Houston, TX, 2017. Copyrighted material.

## CREDITS

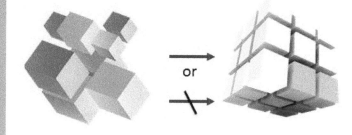

# Test Hypothesis

## Introduction

Business owners want to know how their decisions will impact their business before finalizing any decision. As a result, consultants are often hired to guide them through their decision-making process. Consultants have techniques or methodologies that the client will have confidence in to guide them to a decision or solution to a problem quickly. However, consultants must not overstudy the problem and get caught up in analysis paralysis. Instead, they provide independent and appropriate critical thinking.

The hypothesis development and testing is a tried and true approach method used by many consulting firms and is effective in many engagements (85+%). Hypothesis testing differs from science testing (the scientific method): science deals with "what is" while consultants deal with "what does not yet exist." A hypothesis is an educated guess/hunch.

Hypothesis development or generation asks the question "what if"; hypothesis testing follows it up by saying "if x, then y" with relevant data and analysis. If we keep doing this, we can keep improving the hypothesis. It is a process of "iteration and learning." The definition of the problem and the solution are not separate; we keep refining, reshaping, and sharpening both.

Hypothesis testing uses abductive reasoning. Inductive reasoning starts with data, working backward to form a rule. For example, you look at a set of data and notice when prices increase, demand falls. Deductive reasoning starts with a rule and predicts what you will observe. For example, when price increases, demand decreases. However, abductive reasoning goes from effect to cause—if demand is down, it might be because prices are up. In summary:

- Inductive reasoning: something is operative

- Deductive reasoning proves that something must be

- Abductive reasoning only suggests that something may be

Why is abductive reasoning important to a consultant? First, because there is the possibility that both the problem and solutions are unbounded, sound hypothesis generation is critical. Because the answer is an invented choice rather than discovered truth, the answer can be challenged and requires a persuasive argument.

The consultant must make a compelling case that comes from a data-based hypothesis. Explaining "what is" is essential in building confidence in the recommendation.

## What Is Hypothesis Testing?

Hypothesis testing is a step-by-step process to determine whether a stated hypothesis about a given population is reasonable and probable. Hypothesis testing is used to assess the reasonableness of a hypothesis by using sample data. Hypothesis testing can keep you from wasting time on initiatives that do not give you the best answer to the key question. It can also help you maximize your resources and workforce by focusing them on measures that can produce the most significant effects. Applying it to business decisions is easy once you understand how hypothesis testing works and the steps involved.

For example, Figure 10.1 below shows the relationship between Issue versus Hypothesis versus Evidence Required to prove/disprove the hypothesis.

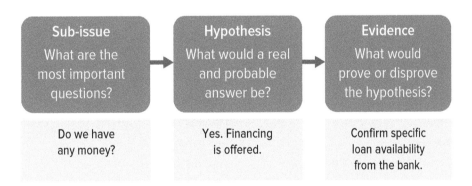

FIGURE 10.1  Component relationships

The first step is to make the overall hypothesis testable; it needs to be rephrased as two mutually exclusive hypotheses. A **null hypothesis** is statistical hypothesis that st ates that there is **no** difference between a parameter and a specific value, or that there is **no** difference between two parameters. An **alternative hypothesis** is a statistical hypothesis that states the existence of a difference between a parameter and a specific value, or states that there is a difference between two parameters. The alternative is basically the hypothesis developed in Chapter 9.

The **null hypothesis** usually states that the population of data is zero. The alternative hypothesis is effectively the opposite and says that the population is not equal to zero (the one found in Figure 10.1

and Table 10.1 under the label Hypothesis). Thus, they are mutually exclusive, and only one can be true. However, one of the two hypotheses will always be true.

Table 10.1 shows an example of the relationships between Issue versus Hypothesis versus Evidence Required.

**TABLE 10.1  Issue, Hypothesis, Evidence**

| Issue | Hypothesis | Evidence Required |
|---|---|---|
| Issue: Good technical decision?<br>• Is the old machine not meeting quality and quantity? | Yes, for the following reasons:<br>• Customer returns are increasing<br>• QA rework increasing<br>• Back orders are increasing | • Time series on returns<br>• Time series on rework<br>• Back orders as a percent of sales<br>• Daily production records |

One null hypothesis for the example in Table 10.1 is that customer returns are the same. The alternative hypothesis is returns are increasing or decreasing. Notice that they are mutually exclusive. Phrases that can be used to create the testing hypothesis are shown in Table 10.2.

**TABLE 10.2  Common Phrases for Hypothesis Testing**

| | |
|---|---|
| Is greater than | Is less than |
| Is above | Is below |
| Is higher than | Is lower than |
| Is longer than | Is shorter than |
| Is bigger than | Is smaller than |
| Is Increased | Is decreased or reduced from |
| Is equal to | Is not equal to |
| Is the same as | Is different from |
| Has not changed from | Has changed from |
| Is the same as | Is not the same as |
| > | < |
| = | ≠ |

## State the Hypothesis of Interest

Before collecting data, the alternative and the null hypotheses must be determined and stated. Before the alternative and null hypotheses can be stated, it is necessary to decide on the desired or expected conclusion of the testing. Generally, the desired conclusion is expressed as the alternative hypothesis. This is true as long as the null hypothesis can include a statement of equality and is mutually exclusive from the alternative hypothesis.

For example, suppose that the consultant is interested in exploring the effects of the amount of study time on test scores. The consultant believes that students who study longer perform better on tests. Specifically, research suggests that students who spend four hours studying for an exam will get a better score than those who study for two hours.

In this case, the hypotheses might be: $H_0$—null hypothesis is the average test scores of students who study 4 hours for the test = the average test scores of those who study 2 hours.

$H_1$—alternative hypothesis is the average test score of students who study 4 hours for the test is greater than the average test scores of those who study 2 hours.

As a result of the statistical analysis, the null hypothesis can be ***rejected*** or ***not rejected***. As a principle of rigorous scientific method, this subtle but important point means that the null hypothesis cannot be ***accepted***.

If the null is rejected, the alternative hypothesis can be accepted. However, if the null is not rejected, we can't conclude that the null hypothesis is true. The rationale is that evidence supporting a hypothesis is inconclusive, but evidence that negates a hypothesis is ample to discredit.

Suppose the results of one study indicate that the test scores of students who study four hours are significantly better than the test scores of students who study two hours.

In that case, the null hypothesis can be rejected because the researcher has found a case when the null is not true and rejected. However, if the study results indicate that the test scores of those who study 4 hours are not significantly better than those who study 2 hours, then the null hypothesis cannot be rejected.

## Other Examples of Stating the Hypothesis

1.  Take the example of sugar with the label 500 gm. As per the above, this represents the scenario when **the statement made is believed to be true in reality**. Thus, it is supposed to be true (based on the given label) that the sugar packet weighs 500 gm. The claim, however, is made that the sugar packet with the label as 500 gm weighs less than 500 gm. Thus, we will need to test hypotheses to determine whether the claim is true or not. Furthermore, the hypothesis testing would need to be done to ascertain the truth about the label mentioned as 500 gm because there is a claim that sugar packets consisted of 480 gm.

    In this scenario, the **null hypothesis** statement is that the weight of packaged sugar is equal to 500 gm. The **alternative hypothesis** statement is that the weight of the sugar packet is less than 500 gm.

2.  Take the example of a claim that running 5 miles a day will reduce 10 pounds of weight within a month. Now, **this is the claim which is required to be proved or otherwise**.

    The **alternative hypothesis** will be stated that "running 5 miles a day will lead to a reduction of 10 pounds of weight within a month."
    The **null hypothesis** will be the opposite of the alternative hypothesis and stated as the fact that "running 5 miles a day does not lead to a reduction of 10 pounds of weight within a month."

3.  Take another example of a claim that the housing price depends upon the average income of people staying in the locality. This is the claim that is required to be proved or otherwise.

    The **alternative hypothesis** will be stated that "housing price depends upon the average income of people staying in the locality."

The **null hypothesis** will be stated that housing price does NOT depend upon the average income of people staying in the locality.

## Develop an Evidence Plan to Test the Hypothesis

The second step in developing a plan to collect the data evidence to prove or disprove the hypothesis is collected by thinking in two dimensions:

- **Method of inquiry:** Questionnaire/interviews, focus groups, research, surveys, observations

- **Source of data:** Internal to the client, client's competition, client's customers, industry reports (IDC, Gartner, major banks), or government statistics (e.g., Census data; Google Earth has great Census data overlays)

Be economical regarding the money and time required in selecting the inquiry method and what source to use—brainstorm possible sources (see Chapter 14.2) to get the necessary data. For example, the data may be from multiple pieces of information and fragments. Set up how you will organize and structure the data collection: Excel files, sources, assumptions, etc. This will be the audit trail so that if someone else uses the data, they can make sense of it. This will help create confidence in the findings and conclusions.

Build a data matrix (see Table 10.3) to keep track of the data collection process, identifying what data is collected and who is collecting it.

TABLE 10.3  **Data Matrix**

| Hypothesis | Null Hypothesis | Evidence | Method of Inquiry | Source | Assigned to |
|---|---|---|---|---|---|
| | | | | | |
| | | | | | |
| | | | | | |

## Collect Evidence

The third step begins with determining the appropriate test statistic, as seen in Table 10.3 in the Method of Inquiry and Source of Data columns. Set up the data collection process based on the inquiry method.

### Determine the Decision Rule for Rejecting the Null Hypothesis

Before data are collected and analyzed, it is necessary to determine under what circumstances the null hypothesis will be rejected or fail to be rejected. The decision rule can be stated in terms of the computed test statistic or probabilistic terms. The same decision will be reached regardless of which method is chosen.

Perform the data collection from the appropriate source(s). Organize the data collected in a spreadsheet, graph, map, etc. A summary of the data collected will be documented in the finding that will be shared with the client.

## Reject or Not Reject the Null Hypothesis

This **fourth step** involves the application of the decision rule. The decision rule allows one to reject or fail to reject the null hypothesis. If one rejects the null hypothesis, the alternative hypothesis can be accepted. However, as discussed earlier, if one fails to reject the null, they can only suggest that the null may be true.

### An Example of a Hypothesis

ABC123 Corporation is a company focused on a stable workforce with minimal turnover. ABC123 has been in business for many years and has more than 10,000 employees. The company has always promoted the idea that its employees stay with them for a very long time, and it has used the following line in its recruitment brochures: "The average tenure of our employees is 20 years."

Since ABC123 isn't quite sure if that statement is still true, a random sample of 100 employees is taken, and the average age turns out to be 19 years with a standard deviation of 2 years. So can ABC123 continue to make its claim, or does it need to make a change?

**State the hypotheses.** $H_0$ (Null hypothesis) = 20 years; $H_1$ (Alternative hypothesis) ≠ 20 years.

**Determine the test statistic.** Since we are testing a population mean that is normally distributed, the appropriate test statistic is Z, $\overline{X}$ = mean of the sample, $\mu$ = mean of the population, $\sigma$ = standard deviation of the sample, and $\eta$ = number in the sample.

**Specify the significance level**. Since the firm would like to keep its present message to new recruits, it selects a fairly weak significance level: the critical values of Z are +1.96 and –1.96.

**State the decision rule**. If the computed value of Z is greater than or equal to +1.96 or less than or equal to –1.96, the null hypothesis is rejected.

**Perform the calculations** on the collected data. The value of Z was calculated to be 2.5.

**Reject or fail to reject the null**. Since 2.5 is greater than 1.96, the null is rejected. The mean tenure is not 20 years; therefore, ABC123 needs to change its statement.

For further reading on statistical concepts and applying them to sets of data, see the Khan Academy: https://www.khanacademy.org/math/statistics-probability

## Document the Findings

Test each hypothesis in Table 10.3 and record the results (extend the table with a **Results** column). Document the analysis by constructing the issue tree with the final sub-issues and hypothesis. Summarize the findings from the testing.

Create a PowerPoint with the following slides:

- Top issue (problem statement)

- Issue analysis tree

- Filled-in expanded data matrix

- Summary of the findings and conclusions

- Problems with data, hypothesis, or access to data, etc.

- Actions you want from the client: approval to proceed with determining recommendations; revise hypothesis or key issue (problem statement) and retest

Present the PowerPoint to the client and move ahead to develop the consultant report or loop back to the appropriate project phase: define the problem or develop a hypothesis.

## CHAPTER SUMMARY

Hypothesis testing has many uses for helping the consultant develop solutions and recommendations for the client. For example, suppose the client is training their outside sales force and wants to know whether a specific sales technique results in a higher close ratio than the methods currently employed. The consultant can take the same steps outlined in this chapter and Chapter 9 to make this determination.

The null hypothesis would be that the new technique has no effect on sales that isn't explained by random chance, while the alternative hypothesis would be that the method has a positive or negative impact.

Finally, suppose the data shows that the technique has an effect and is positive. In that case, the consultant can recommend implementing the new method confidently, knowing it will likely bring the client results.

Hypothesis testing sounds complicated, but it is a simple process, broken down into steps, and it can help consultants recommend better business decisions for their clients.

## QUICK QUIZ

1. What is the alternative hypothesis if a null hypothesis is the average of entering college freshmen = 21?

2. If a null hypothesis is running 5 miles a day does not result in losing 10 pounds of weight within a month, what is the alternative hypothesis?

## QUICK QUIZ ANSWERS

1. The alternative hypothesis is the average age of college freshmen is < 21.

2. The alternative hypothesis is that running 5 miles a day results in losing 5 pounds within a month.

## DISCUSSION QUESTIONS

1. It has been reported that the average credit card debt for college seniors is $5,000. However, the student senate at a large university feels that their seniors have much less debt than this, so how would they prove it?

**2.** The Medical Rehabilitation Education Foundation reports that the average cost of rehabilitation for stroke victims is $24,672. How would you prove or disprove this statement? What would be the null hypothesis and the alternative hypothesis?

## KEY TERMS

**Alternative hypothesis (H₁):** A statement that there is a difference between a parameter and a specific value or a difference between two parameters.

**Null hypothesis (H₀):** A statement that there is no difference between a parameter and a specific value or that there is no difference between two parameters. In this context, the word "null" means a commonly accepted fact.

## END NOTES

Students should use the Khan Academy website (https://www.khanacademy.org/) for lessons in statistics and probability to understand the statistics involved in finding the mean, average, distribution, and data sampling. This is helpful, particularly if you use a survey or focus group to collect data. It will also be helpful to understand the terms often used in government and industry reports.

## REFERENCES

Juncker, Meredith. *How to Test a Hypothesis, 2021.* https://www.wikihow.com/Test-a-Hypothesis#

Kapoor, Amit. *Analytics in Consulting, 2012.* https://www.slideshare.net/amitkaps/analytics-in-consulting

Mahesh. *Everything You Need To Know about Hypothesis Testing—Part I, 2019.* https://towardsdatascience.com/everything-you-need-to-know-about-hypothesis-testing-part-i-4de9abebbc8a

Majaski, Christina. *Hypothesis Testing, 2021.* https://www.investopedia.com/terms/h/hypothesistesting.asp

Mayo, Donna T. *Hypothesis Testing, 2022.* https://www.referenceforbusiness.com/management/Gr-Int/Hypothesis-Testing.html

Minto, Barbara. *The Pyramid Principle: Logic in Writing and Thinking.* Minto International, 1987.

Superior IS. *Issues Analysis, 2019.* Copyrighted material.

## CREDITS

## CHAPTER 11

# Consulting Report

**LEARNING OBJECTIVES**

After studying this chapter, the student will be able to:

- Learn to create recommendations from findings and hypotheses.
- Learn to create and present a consulting report for the client.

Develop Hypothesis        Test Hypothesis        Report Results

IMAGE 11.1

## Introduction

Businesses are often faced with problems, no matter their stage of development. They can usually rely on in-house expertise, but sometimes, their issues or plans require specialized knowledge or training they don't have.

Enter consultants. Businesses hire these professionals to solve problems they can't. Consultants provide expertise and advice to their clients, helping them solve their problems.

One essential tool in a consultant's toolbox is a **consulting report**. These reports provide a detailed examination of an organization's problems and issues and are crucial if the management is serious about solving them.

A comprehensive report is best for consultants to show their skills and expertise.

We'll examine what it is, why it's important, and how to create an effective consulting report.

## What Is a Consulting Report?

A consulting report usually contains the descriptions of the client's problems, an examination or study of those problems from the consultant's perspective, and finally, a set of recommendations or solutions to their problems.

Consulting reports are written for a non-technical audience. They are written in response to a request for research or recommendations to solve a business problem from an organization. The consultant is responsible for ensuring the reader understands the information prepared. The report can be formatted as a PowerPoint slide deck, which reduces the time to create and can be used to present the findings and recommendations. Often, the consultant will have to present their recommendations to executive management or the organization's board of directors.

The consulting report should include the following sections:

- Cover page/title page

- Background information, including staff interviewed, documents reviewed, etc.

- The actionable recommendations and rationale (prioritized)

- The findings

- Other observations

- Conclusions and next steps

- Appendixes

## Why Create a Consulting Report?

Managing a business is challenging, and most business owners and managers have to deal with many different tasks. But unfortunately, few (if any) have the broad set of skills required to solve every problem in their business.

That's why they turn to consultants and consulting agencies who can provide expertise and help solve their issues. These services are necessary for growth since no single business has an in-house solution for everything.

Consulting reports are useful to clients because they give them recommendations and direction. They're helpful to consultants because they allow them to track how their projects are going. In addition, since consulting reports lay out the project in detail, they are the storyboard for the project and show the engagement results. As a result, they can help consultants improve their future performance and ensure better planning for the future.

The consulting report will provide clients with solutions to their problems. Not only that, a consulting report:

- Provides clarity to your client by focusing on defining the key issues related to their problem without using unnecessary jargon or terms.

- Offers an accurate analysis of your client's business-related problems through facts and figures.

- Presents an array of practical and diverse recommendations and solutions for their problems.

- Helps in the decision-making process of their business.

- Acts as a valuable and reliable source of information for future reference.

The benefits of consulting reports are just too good to be sidelined, so you must create one that represents your best work.

## Report Contents

The consulting report should contain the sections detailed below. There is no set length for consulting reports. It greatly depends on project scope and complexity, company size, format, and countless other factors.

Projects can last anywhere from one to six months or longer, and the reports can be of any length. Each section takes up at least one page, and many take up much more. An executive summary shouldn't exceed two pages, even for long reports.

### Cover Page

The cover page should include the project's name, the consultant's name, the client's name, the date of the report, and any logos; clients and consultants.

### Table of Contents

List the sections of your report and note their corresponding page numbers. Additionally, it can include subheadings or subtopics, allowing the readers to skim the table of contents and go to the section that interests them.

### Executive Summary

(Optional, depending on the size of the report. It should be included for large reports.)

This section summarizes the engagement in as few pages as possible. This will give your readers a rough idea of what to expect and emphasize what the report is about. The summary provides a concise explanation of all the important information in the report and highlights analysis, problems, solutions, recommendations, and conclusions.

### Background Information

Background information should include the following:

- Problem or opportunity: Be specific. Include the problem statement.

- Background information: List any items that lead to the problem or related situations.

- Sources of information: List all the people you have interviewed, your research sources, and documents you received from the client.

- Scope of the proposal: Include any restrictions, areas not covered.

- Approach to solution: Describe the process or methodology used to make recommendations.

## Recommendations

Recommendations must be:

- Actionable/doable—they must advise the client on what they should do, what steps need to be taken.

- Specific—ambiguous recommendations are not helpful. The more specific, the better; they must be doable.

- Rationale—reasons for recommendations.

- Timeframe—the order and relative timeframe in which the recommendations should be executed (e.g., now, the first six months, the second year, etc.)

## Findings

Findings should consist of the issue analysis and hypothesis results. The issue analysis chart and/or hypotheses data matrix table should include the following:

- Strategic questions

- Issues

- Sub-issues

- Hypotheses

- Data method, source, and analyses

- Hypothesis test results

- Other observations

## Conclusions

This section briefly explains what has been achieved by the consulting report and summarizes the findings and recommendations. These should describe what things will look like if the recommendations are followed. Conclusions should also include the next steps to acting on the recommendations.

### Appendixes

Include any charts, data tables, research information related to the findings, and recommendations.

See Chapter 14.8 on how to document the engagement from beginning to end. This will ensure you have everything to write the consulting report and maintain an archive for use in other engagements.

## Develop the Report

Remember, the consulting report should solve problems. The client has a problem that needs to be solved. This is the basic purpose of the report and your engagement with the client. So, ensure your report provides a solution the client needs. Write the report in a logical flow, and keep the audience in mind. Be succinct and write in plain English, using a neutral and unbiased tone.

There are several steps to developing the consulting report:

1. Review the issue analysis and related hypothesis (see Chapter 9) to identify items that should be included in the background information.

2. Brainstorm (see Chapter 14.2) conclusions from analysing the findings (Chapter 10).

3. Brainstorm (see Chapter 14.2) actions, results, and benefits based on conclusions.

4. Screen and select the actions for the recommendations.

5. The action results and benefits will become the rationale.

6. Create the report in a PowerPoint format.

When creating the **recommendations**, don't reach for the sky and recommend your ultimate ideal solution. Because reports that include unattainable recommendations will very likely sit on the shelf, gathering dust. What's required is a measured and considered process. Make sure your recommendations aren't pie-in-the-sky but are achievable and doable by the client.

Before you include recommendations in your report, test the waters with the client first. Discuss possible recommendations based on the findings and gauge what's likely to work for the client. The recommendations should be based on where the client is at and what they have for a budget and capabilities to execute. Remember, there is always more than one way up the mountain. Preview a draft copy of the report with key client staff to ensure you do not have words or phrases that could cause great emotion for the client's organization. Different words can be used to get the same point across.

## Present the Report

Here are a few tips for presenting to executives:

- Start with the bottom line—that is why recommendations are presented first.

- Respect their time—start on time; practice your presentation until you can present in the time given, allowing for questions.

- Be prepared to be interrupted—allow for this in your timing.

- Be flexible.

- Be candid.

- Do your homework—who is going to be at the meeting, what is their role, etc.

- Make the connection with the audience and relate recommendations to them.

- Manage all stakeholders in advance.

- Choose meaning over details—explain what any numbers/graphs mean. Please don't leave it to the audience to have to interrupt.

Review Chapter 14.7 on running a successful meeting.

## Rehearse, Rehearse, Rehearse!

Before presenting, run your talk and your slides by a colleague who will serve as an honest coach. Try to find someone who's had success getting ideas adopted at the executive level. Ask for pointed feedback: Is your message coming through clearly and quickly? Are you missing anything your audience is likely to expect?

Sound like a lot of work? It is, but presenting to an executive team is a great honor and can open tremendous doors. If you nail this, people with a lot of influence will become strong advocates for your ideas. This is how you increase the branding of the consulting practice and will bring in more business. See Chapter 13, Going to the Next Level to become a "Trusted Adviser."

## CHAPTER SUMMARY

A **consulting report** is a document containing a **consultant's** expert understanding and advice on a particular subject; for example, a **competitive analysis report** that looks at the strengths and weaknesses of a company's key competitors.

The report contains background information about the project and the client. In addition, it has the findings and most important actionable recommendations. The report should give the client answers to their problem and the next steps to do something about implementing a solution.

As a consultant, your reputation will rest on the quality of your reports. Because even if you've done a great job in every other aspect of the project, your client will ultimately be unhappy if you fail to deliver an excellent report.

The consultant report is the only tangible legacy of the project, so you want that legacy to be a positive one that strengthens rather than diminishes your reputation.

## QUICK QUIZ

1. What is the key source of developing the answer to the client's problem?

2. What is the key attribute of a recommendation?

## QUICK QUIZ ANSWERS

1. What is the key source of developing the answer to the client's problem?

   a. The hypotheses and their results

2. What is the key attribute of a recommendation?

   a. The recommendation must be actionable

## DISCUSSION QUESTIONS

1. Discuss issues that would be included in a consulting report for the Reference Case Study (Chapter 14.9).

2. What are things that should be considered when presenting to executive management?

## KEY TERMS

**Actionable recommendations:** These must advise the client what to do and in enough detail (include steps to be taken) that there is no misunderstanding. They must be specific and not vague or ambiguous.
**Consulting report:** A document containing a consultant's expert understanding and advice on a particular subject.

## END NOTES

There are many good templates to use in developing a consultant's reports. Some selected references are below:

Venngage: https://venngage.com/blog/consulting-report-template/#1

Databox: https://databox.com/dashboard-examples

## REFERENCES

BIT.AI Blog. *Consulting Report: What Is It and How to Create It?* 2021. https://blog.bit.ai/consulting-report/

Paperbell, Team. *4 Simple Steps to an Impactful Consulting Report,* 2022. https://paperbell.com/blog/consulting-report-example/

Štefanović, Davor. *How to Write a Great Business Consulting Report: Best Practices and Report Examples,* 2020. https://databox.com/business-consulting-report

Superior IS. *Project Reports,* 2019. Copyrighted material.

## CREDITS

# Starting a Business

## Introduction

### Starting a Business Introduction

Many people consider forming a business because they see a problem that they believe they could address. Or they have an idea about a product or a service that would benefit people or the community. You have to have a good product or service, and there has to be a "market" or a need for that product or service.

*Do you have the right stuff to have a small business?*

- Do you like people? You get along with almost everyone.

- Are you a self-starter? You do things on your own without someone prodding you.

- Can you lead or influence others? You can get most people to go along when you start something.

- Can you take responsibility? You like to take charge and see them through.

- Are you a good organizer? You like to have a plan before you start. So you are usually the one to get things lined up when the group wants to do something.

- Are you a hard worker? You can keep going as long as it takes to accomplish a task.

- Can you make decisions? You can make up your mind in a hurry if you need to.

- Can people trust what you say? You don't say things you don't mean and that are not valid.

- Can you stick with it? You can decide to do something, and nothing will stop you.

- Do you have good health? You have good health and lots of energy.

- Do you have enough money to live on for six months to a year?

# Forms of Business

There are several forms of businesses to choose from:

## Sole Proprietorship

A **sole proprietorship** is the most common and simplest form of business structure. A sole proprietorship exists when a single individual who owns all of the business's assets engages in business activity without having a formal organization.

A sole proprietor is personally liable for all debts and liabilities. Under a sole proprietorship, there are no legal distinctions between personal debts and business debts, and there is no requirement to file a separate federal income tax return. However, business ownership is nontransferable because an individual cannot transfer his or her tax identification number to another person or entity—a new tax identification number will be required. For similar reasons, the business's life is limited to the life of the sole proprietor.

A sole proprietorship is often operated under the name of the owner. However, suppose a sole proprietorship conducts business under a name other than the surname of the individual owner. In that case, where a business premise is maintained, it is necessary to file an "Assumed Name Certificate" (commonly referred to as a "DBA certificate") with the office of the county clerk. If no business premise is maintained, then an assumed name certificate should be filed in all counties where business is conducted under the assumed name. More information is available on registering an assumed name certificate with your local county clerk's office.

## Partnership

In a **partnership**, each individual contributes money, labor, skill, or property and expects an agreed-upon return for the contribution. There are two kinds of partnerships, general and limited, with the essential difference being in the extent of liability and the degree of power.

## General Partnership

A general partnership is fairly simple and relatively inexpensive to set up. Bookkeeping and tax returns need a CPA. Losses can be written off against personal tax liability. However, all partners are liable for debts or negligence of any other partner. Most states require registration and annual reports.

## Limited Partnership

Here, the partners' liability is limited to their original investment. The general partners manage the enterprise, and the limited partners have no power. The tax benefits flow through to the individual's tax return.

If you are going into business with others, agree in writing before starting up about what will happen if:

- The principal dies;

- The principal wishes to sell their interest;

- Other principals want one principal out;

- An offer to buy a firm is made by outsiders;

- Checks are drawn on a business bank account;

- Loans, or other binding commitments, are made on behalf of the business;

- Officers and board of directors are to be chosen.

## Limited Liability Company

A **limited liability lompany** (LLC) is neither a corporation nor a partnership; instead, it is a distinct entity type. It is an unincorporated business entity that shares some aspects of Subchapter S corporations and limited partnerships but has more flexibility than more traditional business entities.

The owners of an LLC are called "members." An LLC may have one or more members.

A member can be an individual, a partnership, a trust, and any other legal entity. However, unlike the partnership, where the critical element is the individual, the essence of an LLC is the entity, which requires more formal requirements in terms of registration.

The limited liability company is designed to provide its owners with limited liability and pass-through tax advantages without the restrictions imposed on Subchapter S corporations and limited partnerships.

Generally, the liability of the members is limited to their investment, and they may enjoy the pass-through tax treatment afforded to partners in a partnership. As a result of federal tax classification rules, an LLC can achieve structural flexibility and favorable tax treatment. Nevertheless, persons contemplating forming an LLC should consult with an attorney about whether this structure suits their business needs.

## For-Profit Corporation

A corporation is a legal person with limited liability, central management, perpetual duration, and ease of transferability of ownership interests. The owners of a corporation are called shareholders. The persons who manage the business and affairs are called directors. A **for-profit corporation** must register with a particular state's secretary of state.

Choosing the best management structure for your corporation, should you pursue this formation, is a decision you should make under the advisement of an attorney. Please note that what is referred to as an "S" corporation is not a matter of state corporate law but rather a federal tax election. A for-profit corporation elects to be taxed as an "S" corporation by filing for this status with the Internal Revenue Service. You should contact the IRS and/or competent tax counsel regarding the decision to elect to file as an "S" corporation, which requires more formal requirements in terms of registration for federal tax purposes. Corporations are subject to state and federal taxes.

## The Best Form for Small Business

The Limited Liability Company is generally the easiest and best form for starting a small business. It requires minimal paperwork to set up and gives you the protection of a corporation.

# Business Plan

After deciding on a business form, the next step is to create a **business plan**.

Creating a comprehensive business plan is a crucial process. The idea of writing a business plan may not seem important; however, it ultimately serves many vital purposes. It will serve to outline the primary purpose of your business, its structure, its financing, and its advantages over other market competitors. A solid business plan can be a framework for your company's mission and support when applying for financing.

Items that are included in a business plan:

**Business Name**

**Executive summary.** The product or service your company will sell; to whom the product or service will be sold; how much this will cost; and how long it will take to become profitable. Keep it simple.

**Business setup and structure.** Start with describing the company's business, legal, and leadership structure. Follow this with a discussion of the company's management approach, hiring process, and office and equipment needs. Finally, include a list of the necessary licenses and permits that will be obtained.

**Strategic financial plan.** Outline how much money the business will need and where the support will come from. Include a breakdown of the monthly budget and cash flow for the first year. Include detailed information on the current market and projected customer demands; pricing strategy; available financial support; anticipated financial support; costs associated with development, production, office space, employee salaries, equipment purchase, etc.; anticipated timeline for marketing; goals for profitability. If your business seeks financing, you will probably be asked to provide income statements demonstrating sound financial accountability. Provide a stated goal for when the company will be profitable and the return on the investment.

**Development and regulatory process outline.** Provide a timeframe demonstrating the time it will take to build, produce, and generate the business. Include a breakdown of any risk and explain why and how that will be overcome.

**Marketing plan.** Provide information regarding the ideal customer, how the ideal customer will be reached, and when this will occur. Provide information on the pricing strategy and why consumers will buy the product or service. Provide an overview of how marketing and outreach will serve to promote your business so that consumers become a reality. Explain how the product will be marketed to demonstrate a competitive edge over the industry's other similar product or service providers. Finally, explain the expenses involved in selling the product and services.

**Biographies.** For all the people on the team, include biographies that demonstrate the team members' education, experience, skills, and expertise are in line with the business's mission.

**Launch and delivery plan.** Discuss where the business is going. Inform readers of how investors will get money out of business and the return rate on the investment will eventually look. Include a discussion of whether the company could finally be public and what would be at risk.

# Checklist to Start a Small Business

## Checklist to Start a Consulting Business

There are several steps involved in starting a consulting business. Don't get discouraged by the long list that follows. Complete one section at a time, then the next, etc.

1. Develop a business. (*The E-Myth* by Michael E. Gerber is a great resource.)

   - 1.1 Determine legal structure (Sole Proprietor, LLC Limited Partnership)

   - 1.2 Develop the ownership structure

   - 1.3 Develop business management structure

     - Operations (finance, AP, AR, etc.)

     - Service development

     - Project management

     - Marketing

   - 1.4 Business funding

     - Internal funding—friends and family

     - External funding—venture capitalist, angel networks

   - 1.5 Identify business locations

   - 1.6 Develop compensation structure

   - 1.7 Develop a business strategy

   - 1.8 Develop pricing strategy

   - 1.9 Financial analysis

     - Balance sheet

     - Statements

     - Cash flow projections

     - Break-even analysis

2. Implement a business structure.

   - 2.1 Set up legal entities. Get an Employer Identification Number (EIN) from the IRS, available online. (Make sure the name you have chosen is available; Google it)

   - 2.2 Open bank accounts with company name

   - 2.3 Hire a lawyer (optional)

   - 2.4 Implement a compensation plan

   - 2.5 Implement a benefits plan (optional)

   - 2.6 Hire/identify an accounting firm/PA/CPA

   - 2.7 Develop key policies and processes

3. Develop a technology and communications infrastructure.

   - 3.1 Select a technology infrastructure.

     - Platforms—cloud, local server, or remote hosted

     - Email, file storage

     - Accounting package (QuickBooks, QuickBooks Online)

     - Local Area Network—wired or wireless

   - 3.2 Select tools—office software/hardware, backup, etc.

   - 3.3 Develop standards:

     - Naming conventions

     - Document format

4. Develop a marketing plan.

   - 4.1 Identify market attractiveness.

     - Growth rates

     - Identify potential customers

     - Identify industry/market segmentation

     - Identify sales channels

     - Identify competitors

   - 4.2 Identify trade shows/seminars to participate in.

5. Implement a marketing and sales plan.

   - 5.1 Attend trade shows

   - 5.2 Develop marketing collateral

   - 5.3. Develop a sales plan, tasks, and responsibilities

   - 5.4 Execute the sales plan. Use the SPIN® approach for each contact in your network

6. Develop a business plan.

   - 6.1 Business name

   - 6.2 Executive summary

   - 6.3 Business setup and structure

   - 6.4 Strategic financial plan

   - 6.5 Development and regulatory process outline

   - 6.6 Marketing plan

   - 6.7 Biographies

   - 6.8 Launch and delivery plan

7. Develop a knowledge base. Build databases of:

   - 7.1 Potential customers: names, addresses, phone, email, etc.

   - 7.2 Competitors: names, addresses, phone numbers, competitive posture

   - 7.3 Information resources: websites, ISO standards, white papers, articles, etc.

   - 7.4 Tools/products: tool name, usefulness rating, citations for where/how used, etc.

   - 7.5 Work example: actual work examples/experiences where organizations have already served a customer or similar work for a previous company

8. Develop and implement a staffing plan.

   - 8.1 Identify staffing needs

   - 8.2 Hire staff

   - 8.3 Staff projects

   - 8.4 Review staff performance

# Running the Small Business

## Checklist for Running a Business

Many steps are involved in running a business (e.g., consulting). So don't get discouraged by the long list that follows.

- Create processes for everything—dumb it down, allowing the hiring of reduced-skill employees or contractors. Spend time working "on" your business, not "in" it!

- Create process documentation as if you were going to franchise the business—a series of simple task writeups; don't leave questions unanswered.

- Create a detailed budget and monitor/manage against this on a weekly/monthly basis

- Rent minimal space and buy minimal equipment, etc. Use services: Office Depot, Kinko's, etc.

- Set up a business bank account.

- Buy letterhead stationery, business cards with the same colors, logo, etc.—branding.

- Buy laptop/Chromebook with Cloud version of MS Office, QuickBooks, Google Workspace.

- Buy good-quality all-in-one laser printer (fax, scan, copy, print).

- Create a business/marketing plan.

- Setup: email, eFax, eStorage, ePhone accounts; website; business Facebook page; business LinkedIn page; and consider an Instagram business page.

- Outsource any service jobs: accounting, clerical, printing, binding, etc.

- Obtain business liability insurance.

- **Remember, cash is king; hang on to it!**

### Where Should I Work?

A home office has low overhead expenses, flexibility, and no rush-hour nightmares, and your home office space will most likely be tax-deductible. But will family interfere? Is it quiet and separate from the rest of the house? Do you need to interact in person with the clients much?

### What Do I Charge?

- Your hourly rate is so high that no one could ever afford you.

- Your hourly rate is so low that no one will take you seriously.

- Call a consultant/contractor in your area and get quotes for helping one of your "clients."

- Try to use fixed-price projects where possible; include all billable hours plus profit margin (25%), and the client will pay direct expenses at cost.

- Starting point range for hourly rate: Current salary / 960 +20% to 3 x Current Salary /1800.

### Do I Need a Contract?

You need a proposal/letter of agreement (LOA) with general provisions. (See the example below; it has standard last page that you can use with all proposals.) The proposal should contain the following:

- Business services proposed

- Client's background and his or her issue (problem statement)

- Your approach to assisting with the client's issue

- Schedule and payment (ask for 25% to 50% up front) plus expenses reimbursed

- One-page General Provisions include confidentiality, independent contractor status, intellectual property, liabilities

- Signature for you and the client to agree

## Sample General Provisions for a Proposal/Letter of Agreement

Our work for you is confidential, and we will preserve the confidential nature of any appropriately designated proprietary information received from you or developed during our work for you.

Either party may use the name of the other for advertising or promotional purposes with prior permission. It is understood that work products resulting from this assignment are intended for your internal use and are not to be used in whole or in part outside your organization. External use of our work products will require our prior written approval. All work products approved for external use will contain a notice describing or limiting the conditions under which the work products can be distributed and/or used.

Our work will be performed on a best-efforts basis consistent with the degree of skill and care customarily exercised by consulting firms performing services of a similar nature. Our total liability arising from or in connection with the results of our work or any recommendations made according to this agreement shall not exceed the total compensation paid to us. As a result, you agree to release, indemnify, and hold us harmless from and against any costs or liability in excess (including claims against us by third parties). We shall not be liable for any indirect, consequential, special, or incidental losses or damages.

This agreement (including resolution of any disputes arising hereunder) will be governed by and interpreted according to the laws of the State of Texas.

| Client | Consultant |
|---|---|
| By: _____ | By: _____ |
| Name: _____ | Name: _____ |
| Title : _____ | Title: _____ |
| Date : _____ | Date : _____ |

## CHAPTER SUMMARY

Know yourself and your capabilities: interests, energy level, time limitations, selling, and delivery. Know your dollar situation. You may need to carry yourself for one year or more. Assume zero income, many blind avenues, and first assignments do not necessarily pay well. It will probably be necessary to cut the price to get a foot in the door to build a client list. No one wants to be your first job—later, clients are more concerned with what you can do for them than how much you charged for the last engagement. Typically, consultants are hired for specific needs and expertise to compensate for employees who companies cannot keep on staff.

Keep appearances up, costs down. Buy the new suit, use quality stationery and business cards, some type of answering service, or a Google Voice phone number, and create a simple website or business Facebook page and LinkedIn business profile.

Setup a Google Workspace or Microsoft 365 business account to store documents, presentations, etc. Obtain a URL for your website, email addresses, etc. But operate "out of the spare bedroom or kitchen table" initially to conserve all the cash you can.

Develop a business and marketing plan and start executing it.

## QUICK QUIZ

1. What is king when running a small business?

2. What are the primary forms of a small business?

## QUICK QUIZ ANSWERS

1. What is king when running a small business? Cash.

2. What are the primary forms of a small business? Sole proprietor (DBA), partnership, limited liability company

## DISCUSSION QUESTIONS

1. Discuss why starting a business may not be the right thing for you.

2. Why is a business plan essential?

## KEY TERMS

**For-profit corporation:** A corporation is a legal person with limited liability, central management, perpetual duration, and ease of transferring ownership interests. The owners of a corporation are called shareholders. The persons who manage the business and affairs are called directors. A for-profit corporation must register with a particular state's secretary of state.

**Limited liability company:** The limited liability company (LLC) is neither a corporation nor a partnership; instead, it is a distinct type of entity. It is an unincorporated business entity that shares some aspects of Subchapter S corporations and limited partnerships but has more flexibility than more traditional business entities.

**Partnership:** In a partnership, each individual contributes money, labor, skill, or property and expects an agreed-upon return for the contribution.

**Sole proprietorship:** A sole proprietorship is the most common and simplest business structure. A sole proprietorship exists when a single individual who owns all of the business's assets engages in business activity without having to have a formal organization.

**Business plan:** Serves many essential purposes. It will serve to outline your business's primary purpose, structure, financing, and advantages over other market competitors. A solid business plan can be a framework for your company's mission and support when applying for financing.

## END NOTES

Michael Gerber, *The E-Myth Revisited: Why Most Small Businesses Don't Work and What to Do About It*. Harper Business, 2004.

*The E-Myth Revisited* by Michael Gerber is one of the most recommended books for people who want to start a business, if not *the* most recommended. If you're going to create your own business, you must read this book. Although I have to say that I generally disliked the writing style. Michael also writes poetry, and it somewhat influenced how he wrote this book; there is a lot of storytelling, which made it difficult for me at times to get what he was trying to convey.

The following summary from *The E-Myth Revisited* by Michael Gerber is meant to be concise, high-level concepts and not to try to re-create the whole book. Therefore, this summary is a bunch of notes and lessons paraphrased or quoted directly from the book and does not contain my thoughts.

- The E-Myth (or "Entrepreneurial Myth") believes that entrepreneurs start small businesses by risking capital to make a profit. This is not so. The real reasons people start businesses have little to do with entrepreneurship.

- Your business is nothing more than a distinct reflection of who you are. If your thinking is sloppy, your business will be sloppy. If you are disorganized, your business will be disorganized. If you are greedy, your employees will be greedy, giving you less and less of themselves and always asking for more. If the information about what needs to be done in your business is limited, your business will reflect that limitation.

- People who are exceptionally good in business aren't so because of what they know, but their insatiable need to learn more.

- The problem with most failing businesses I've encountered is not that their owners don't know enough about finance, marketing, management, and operations—they don't. Still, those things are easy enough to learn. But they spend their time and energy defending what they *think* they know. The greatest businesspeople I've met are determined to get it right no matter what the cost.

- The great ones I have known seem to possess an intuitive understanding that the only way to reach something higher is to focus on the multitude of seemingly insignificant, unimportant, and uninteresting things that make up every business. (And that make up every life, for that matter!)

## REFERENCES

Gerber, Michael. *The E-Myth Revisited*. New York: HarperCollins, 1995.

Holtz, Herman. *How to Succeed as an Independent Consultant*. New York. John Wiley & Sons, 1988.

Shenson, Howard L. *Complete Guide to Consulting Success*. Wilmington, DE: Enterprise Publishing, 1991.

Small Business Administration. Small Business Readiness Assessment, 2022. https://eweb1.sba.gov/cams/training/business_primer/assessment.htm

# Going to the Next Level

*The way to be a great consultant is to care about your client.*
—DAVID MAISTER ET AL., THE TRUSTED ADVISOR

---

**LEARNING OBJECTIVES**

---

After reading this chapter, students will be able to:

- Discuss the four steps in the evolution of the client-consultant relationship: subject matter expert, subject matter expert plus related field, valued resource, and trusted consultant.

- Discuss the four types of personal relationships between client and consultant and the issues that are solved in each relationship.

- Discuss the four traits needed by consultants to become trusted.

- Discuss the variables of trust and the trust equation.

- Use the trust equation to determine a consultant's relationship with a client.

- Discuss the five stages in the process of developing trust between the client and the consultant.

## How to Move Beyond Being a "Hired Gun"

None of us begins our career as a consultant knowing where it will take us. In addition, consultants all aspire for greater and greater responsibility. Consultants hope to be appreciated for the advice they bring to their clients. However, consultants usually begin as a "hired gun," performing a specific task or maybe a single service that uses their special skills (see Figure 13.1). The consultants may be great at what they do, but their activities are limited to the immediate needs of their client. This is the lowest level, the subject matter expert or process expert level.

If a consultant is successful in meeting the needs of the client as a **subject matter expert** (the most basic level; i.e., the "hired gun"), the client may increase trust in their abilities. This may or may not be in the consultant's original subject matter area. When this happens, the client recognizes that the consultant may be able to solve problems beyond their original subject matter expertise. The client may in fact call

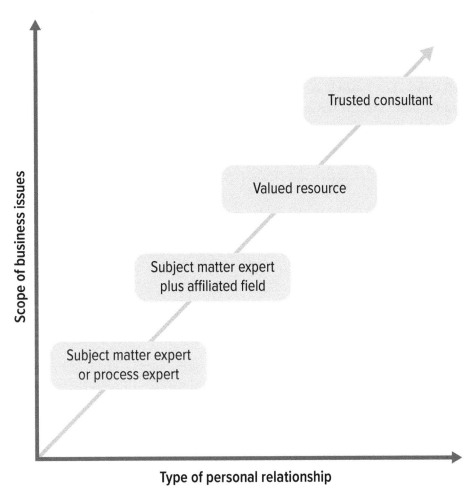

FIGURE 13.1  The evolution of a client-consultant relationship

upon us to help define the problems that the client seeks to solve. This is the next level up, the subject matter expert plus affiliated field level.

If the consultant is successful in meeting the problem-solving needs of the client, then the client may consider asking the consultant for advice solving strategic-level problems not only in their subject matter expertise. The consultant starts to offer advice proactively and to be looking at issues within the client's whole organization.

If the consultant is successful in meeting the strategic problem-solving needs of the client, then the client may consider asking the consultant for advice on all matters personal and professional. The consultant has become the go-to person when an issue arises. The issues that the consultant is asked for advice on are beyond just the organization. The issues may involve a personal dimension. Working at this level requires the consultant to master not only the subject matter expertise, but organizational and interpersonal skills. This is the final level, the **trusted consultant** (or adviser) level.

The relationships shown in Figure 13.1 are a function of the business issues, but the client and consultant work on as well the personal relationship between them. The successful consultant is one who can shift comfortably and quickly between the types of relationships, depending upon business issues.

The successful consultant is one who places a higher value on maintaining and enhancing the relationship between the client and the consultant, than a particular outcome of the engagement that the consultant is completing for the client.

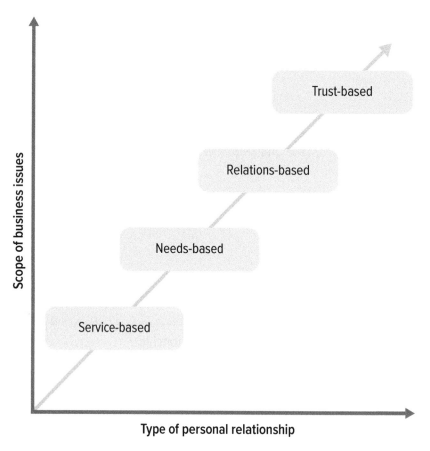

FIGURE 13.2  Client-consultant relationship as a function of issues and personal relationship

## Traits Needed by Consultants to Become Trusted

Looking at Figures 13.1 and 13.2, we can see various traits are common to all successful consultants. Successful consultants do the following:

- Focus on the client, not themselves

- Listen without prejudging

- Inquire without assuming an answer

- View client as coequal

- Strengthen to control their own ego

- Focus on the client as a person, not a placeholder

- Focus on the problem, not cool technical solutions

- Focus on developing new ways to help the client

- Focus on doing the right thing

- Are self-actualized

- Recognize that methodologies, processes, etc., are tools. They are only useful when they help the client

- Show the client that they are dedicated to them by serving them

- Recognize that while the business life and the personal life are different, frequently business life and personal life are two sides of the same coin

The traits show that success for the consultant comes to the consultant who chooses not to make success the primary goal. The way to be a successful consultant is to care about the client. Caring about the client begins with developing a trusting relationship between the client and the consultant. There are three areas that a consultant must master. The areas are earning trust, building relationships, and giving advice (see Figure 13.3). The areas are interrelated, with all beginning with the consultant earning the trust of the client.

FIGURE 13.3  Skills needed to create and use trust

## The Components of Trust and the Trust Equation

The first step for a consultant developing a relationship with a client begins with earning **trust**. Trust must be established by both the consultant and the client. This is summarized in the "trust equation" found in Figure 13.4:

For the equation:

T = Trustworthiness
C = Credibility
R = Reliability
I = Intimacy
S = Self-absorption

Let's look at each of these variables and how they are related.

$$T = \frac{C + R + I}{S}$$

FIGURE 13.4  The trust equation

## Credibility

The first variable contributing to trustworthiness is credibility. **Credibility** is often the most easily established variable. As a business professional, a consultant demonstrates technical ability and achievements by their résumé. In the résumé, someone can find a consultant's academic achievements and their achievements in the business world. However, credibility goes beyond a consultant's technical achievements. Included in credibility is a consultant's "presence." A consultant's presence is how a consultant comes across to their client. It is how a consultant looks, talks, acts, and reacts to their client. Credibility is broken into both emotional and rational components. When creating credibility, the consultant must be patient. Credibility takes time to establish.

At an emotional level, if a consultant comes into contact with the client, whether it be via teleconference or face-to-face, and the consultant is not dressed in a businesslike fashion, the client immediately knows that the consultant is not serious and not credible. Likewise, if a consultant comes to the client and is not articulate and confident, the client immediately knows that the consultant is not serious and not credible. If the consultant is nervous and unconfident, the client immediately knows that the consultant is not serious and not credible.

At a rational level, if a consultant comes into contact with the client, whether it be via teleconference or face-to-face, and the consultant's information is not accurate or complete, the client immediately knows that the consultant is not serious and is not credible. And if the client recognizes that the consultant is not being honest, not telling the truth, they immediately know that the consultant is not serious and not credible. If the consultant has not demonstrated that they are technically competent and experienced (as per the consultant's résumé), the client immediately knows that the consultant is not serious and is not credible.

A consultant is more credible when they:

1. Tell the truth. Mark Twain once said, "Always tell the truth. You don't have to remember what you said."

2. Don't tell lies, or in fact even exaggerate. Mark Twain also once said, "Truth is the most valuable thing we have."

3. Avoid saying thanks: it might even be construed as an exaggeration or a lie.

4. Use body language when speaking. Look the client in the eye.

5. Before meeting the client, send a brief résumé to the client to establish your credentials.

6. Relax! You, the consultant, know more than you think you do.

7. Do your homework! Not coming prepared to a meeting sends a signal that you are not serious about the meeting.

8. Love the topic that you are meeting with the client about. The consultant's passion for the topic comes across in body language.

## Reliability

The next variable is reliability. **Reliability** means consultant is dependable, consistent and do what they say they will do. Thus, reliability depends upon the number of times the consultant interacts with the client. The first time a consultant meets a client, the client has nothing on which to base the consultant's reliability. If, after five meetings between the consultant and the client, the consultant has fulfilled their commitments from earlier meetings, the client now has some history on which to base reliability. Reliability also depends upon the little touches, such as sending out an agenda prior to a meeting. Reliability also depends upon knowing and understanding the client's business situation.

A consultant is more reliable when they:

- Make commitments to the client and then follow up on them quickly. These commitments can be little things like sending out minutes the next day from a meeting.

- Send out meeting materials in advance so the client can review the materials before the meeting. This means sending out not only the agenda but any supporting information.

- Ask the client for input to the agenda. By asking for input, the consultant is giving the client ownership of the meeting.

- Make sure all meetings have an agenda that includes clear goals. Typically, these include any action items completed from prior meetings.

- Reconfirm a day in advance of a meeting the time, the location (videoconference, teleconference, or face-to-face), and the agenda.

## Intimacy

The next variable is **intimacy**. The most common failure for a consultant when building trust is the lack of intimacy. Business is all about people! Frequently, though, consultants try to maintain a distance from their clients. Clients are people. They have emotions. It should not come as a surprise that successful consultants seeking to build a connection engage with the emotional side of a client.

A consultant is more intimate when they:

- Are not afraid to be open with the client.

- Ask themselves what they would do if they were the client.

- Lay out some questions that they feel the client can easily answer.

- Try to create intimacy, it is usually easier for the consultant to start and make the first move. Simple things like traditional social greetings such as "How are you today?" go a long way to establish intimacy.

- Intimacy is not just candor. It is about telling the truth.

### Self-absorption

**Self-absorption** is the variable that reduces trust faster than any of the others. There are many signs of self-absorption: selfishness; a need to appear on top of things; always wanting to be right; and not wanting to appear ignorant.

A consultant is less self-absorbed when they:

- Involve the client in the consulting project.

- Engage the client by asking open-ended questions about the consulting proposal.

- Follow the adage, "You have two ears and one month. Use them in that ratio." In other words, "Seek to understand and be understood."

- Focus on defining the problem. A problem well defined is half solved.

- Are being honest and say they do not know, when they do not know. Follow this up by committing to see if there is an answer.

- Listen to the client without distractions and with all their attention.

- Add value to the conversation by listening to the client finish and then adding value.

## The Process of Developing Trust

The consultant needs to know the process for developing trust. There are five steps (stages) to developing trust. The consultant follows the steps shown in Figure 13.5 to develop that trust.

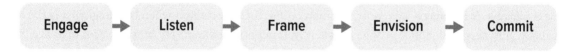

FIGURE 13.5  Steps to developing trust

### 1. Engagement

The first step in developing trust is **engagement**. The consultant has met with the client, and they are beginning the process of developing trust between them. At this point, the client is starting to realize that the consultant has something to offer. And now, the consultant has earned the right to talk and learn about the client. Engaging requires the consultant to have the skill to be recognized.

### 2. Listening

The second step in developing trust is for the client and the consultant to **listen** to each other. At this point, the client is starting to realize that the consultant is hearing and understanding what they are saying. Consequently, the consultant earns the right to propose a problem statement. Listening requires the consultant to have the skill to understand someone.

### 3. Framing

The third step in developing trust is **framing** not only the problem but all the issues that impact on the problem. At this juncture, the client is realizing that the consultant understands the problems and issues involved with their problem. So now the consultant is framing (creating) the problem statements and hypotheses required to solve a problem. It is at this point in the process that the client begins to recognize that the consultant is bringing value to them. Framing requires the consultant to have the skill to create something new and the courage to present it.

### 4. Envisioning

The fourth step in developing trust—**envisioning**—is a joint effort on the part of the client and consultant. In the third step, there are problem solutions and hypotheses created. In the fourth step, the client and the consultant are ready to select a possible solution to the problem. Together they must understand: 1) Does the solution really solve the problem? 2) What does the solution look like? and 3) How will we know the solution solves the problem? Envisioning requires the consultant to have the skills of collaboration and creating a solution with someone.

### 5. Commitment

The fifth step in developing trust is **commitment**. In this step, the client and the consultant commit to implementing the solution. Without this commitment, no further action can be taken. Commitment requires the consultant to have the skill to generate enthusiasm.

## Quick Quiz

1. What are the four steps in the evolution of the client-consultant relationship?

   a. subject matter expert

   b. subject matter expert plus related field

   c. valued resource

   d. trusted consultant

   e. all of the above

2. What are the variables of the trust equation?

   a. trustworthiness

   b. credibility

**c.** reliability

**d.** self-absorption

**e.** all of the above

## Quick Quiz Answers

**1.** all of the above

**2.** all of the above

**CHAPTER SUMMARY**

The key for a consultant to succeed is technical mastery and the ability to work with clients in such a way that the client trusts the consultant. This chapter introduced you to the ideas required to move beyond being a pair of hands, how to earn the trust and confidence of a client. Additionally, this chapter introduced the four steps in the evolution of the client-consultant relationship: subject matter expert; subject matter expert plus related field; valued resource; and trusted consultant. We also discussed the four types of personal relationships between the client and consultant and the issues that are solved in each relationship. This chapter focused on the traits needed by consultants to become trusted. We also introduced the variables of trust and the trust equation. Also discussed was the process of developing trust between the client and the consultant.

**DISCUSSION QUESTIONS**

**1.** Discuss the evolution of the client-consultant relationship from subject - matter expert (SME) to trusted consultant. For each level, include in your discussion both the scope of business issues addressed and the types of personal relationships.

**2.** Discuss the five stages in the process of developing trust between the client and the consultant. How would you use this with a client?

**KEY TERMS**

**Subject matter expert:** A person or consultant that has in-depth knowledge of a specific area of business and can provide clients with a particular service.

**Valued resource:** A person or consultant that has proven to add value-added services.

**Trusted consultant:** A consultant that has become the go-to person for an organization and is involved in the strategic problem-solving needs of the client.

**Service-based relationship:** A relationship with a client that is transactional and is based on consultant providing a specific service.

**Needs-based relationship:** A relationship based on the consultant and client determining the client's need and a solution to it working together.

**Relations-based relationship:** A relationship based on the client-consultant business relation and is not transactional.

**Trust-based relationship:** A relationship based on mutual trust between the client and the consultant who is considered more than a valued resource.

**Trust:** Credibility + reliability + intimacy divided by self-adsorption

**Credibility:** Knowledge based on demonstrated, tested and documented abilities over time.

**Reliability:** Means a consultant is both dependable and consistent in what they do over time.

**Intimacy:** Seeking to build a connection to the emotional side of a client.

**Self-adsorption:** Demonstrating selfishness, a need to appear on top of things, always wanting to be right, and not wanting to appear ignorant.

**Engagement:** The process of developing trust between the client and consultant.

**Listening:** The procession of the skill to deeply understand the client and their needs.

**Framing:** Creating the problem statement, related issues and the environment.

**Envisioning:** The skill of imaging a solution in collaboration with the client.

**Commitment:** The skill and relationship to stick to solving a client's problem and creating enthusiasm for all the stakeholders involved

## REFERENCE

Maister, David H., Charles H. Green, and Robert M. Galford. *The Trusted Advisor*. New York: Simon & Schuster, 2004.

## CREDITS

## CHAPTER 14

# Resources: Consulting Tools, Techniques, and Frameworks

**LEARNING OBJECTIVES**

After reading this chapter, students will be able to:

- Make use of these tools, techniques, and frameworks to perform a business consulting assignment.

- Sample case HT Fitness.

## 14.1 Introduction

This chapter documents several tools and techniques used in various aspects of business consulting.

- Brainstorming

- Data flow diagrams (DFD)

- Multiple-Criteria Decision Analysis (MCDA)

- Minto principles, including MECE

- Running successful meetings

- Documenting a consulting project (client/project wiki)

- HT Fitness case for study

- Fishbone/Ishikawa diagram

## 14.2 Brainstorming

The purpose of brainstorming is to involve a group of people in generating ideas. The group effort is very effective in creating ideas, team building, improving communication, and educating all involved.

Roles include the following:

- Participants. The people who will be involved in generating ideas. They will respect each and every idea of others and contribute their own.

- Recorder. The person assigned to list the ideas on a whiteboard, flipchart paper, or laptop with a projector and record all votes, etc. This person will have primary responsibility for taking notes, producing a report of the group's results, and distributing copies to all participants.

- Moderator. The person assigned to start and close the session on time, maintain the pace of the session, resolve conflicts, stop irrelevant discussions, rule on procedural matters, and ensure everyone gets to participate.

## Session Procedure

1. The moderator is as precise as possible in stating the topic to be discussed. Then, the moderator asks each participant to contribute one idea in rotation around the table or to pass (participant says "pass").

2. Each participant explains their idea in enough detail to ensure that the group understands before it is added to the list. There are no "bad or stupid ideas."

3. The recorder adds each idea to the whiteboard, flipchart, or laptop with a projector so that all participants may see what has been contributed. The participant's initials will be placed next to the idea for future reference.

4. When all ideas have been presented (i.e., a round when all participants have "passed"), the moderator asks if there are duplicate ideas on the board. The participants decide on the duplicates (voting if necessary) and consolidate the list. Discussion is encouraged to ensure that all unique ideas are recorded (they may need to be restated).

5. Participants are asked to identify all "opposite" ideas. Participants present pros and cons. After a reasonable period of discussion, the moderator calls for a vote. A simple majority vote determines which idea is kept on the list.

6. The moderator calls for a vote on each remaining idea. Participants vote after a short discussion of the pros and cons of that idea. If the vote is greater than 50% of all the participants, the idea is kept to be addressed later. Any participant may ask for a rebuttal of the vote and try to convince other participants of an idea's merit, and then another vote will be taken.

7. The remaining ideas are assigned to appropriate people for follow-up and reporting back to the group.

## Ground Rules

Ground rules include the following:

- One idea or pass, in rotation, per turn

- Be creative; quantity is desirable during idea generation

- *NO* commentary or judgment during idea generation (good or bad)

- Majority rules

## 14.3 Data Flow Diagrams

A definition of a Data Flow Diagram (DFD) is a picture of the flows of data through a system of any kind showing the external entities, which are sources or destinations of data, the processes that transform data, and the places where data is stored. The key benefit of data flow diagramming is its concentration of data—data stores and data flows—to divide a system into processes.

**A.** Data flows and data stores are groups of data items that describe external entities or business events of particular importance to the system. Data flows are collections of items **in motion** between a user and a process, between processes, or between a process and a data store. Data stores are a collection of items **at rest** between processes on different time cycles. Processes are system actions that collect input data and prepare output data or transform data from one form to another. Separate processes may be necessary for a system because of differences in timing between data collection and analysis, differences in the origin of input data flow, differences in the destinations of output flows, or changes in data sequence in a transformation. Such processes may be decomposed further if their transformation is so complex as to require subdivisions for clarity of understanding. This further decomposition or breakdown of the process is called explosion.

**B.** Identifying processes can begin with recognizing that a data store will have at least one process that maintains it and one process that uses it. If data with a data store is collected from different users or at other times, there will be several maintaining processes. Likewise, if the data participates in several reports or communications, then there will be several using processes.

**C.** The analytical process begins with a list of the users—people, institutions or other systems, and their data flows with the system. User data flows will be significant inputs recording events of interest to the system or important outputs. The objective of the first-level diagram is to chart the system as a black box showing its inputs and their sources and its outputs, and their recipients.

### Data Flow General Information

Below is a first-level data flow diagram (DFD) for a typical non-profit organization. The system we are looking at is the organization as a whole.

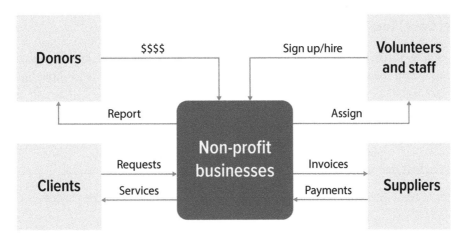

FIGURE 14.1  First-level Data Flow Diagram with four external entities identified

## Data Flow Naming Standards

**A.** Name each data flow uniquely.

**B.** Name the data flow as it applies to the whole data flow, not just to its major component.

**C.** Use meaningful and descriptive names.

**D.** Do not group disparate items into one data flow when they should not be treated as a whole.

**E.** Hyphenate data flow names and use initial capitalization in the title.

**F.** Choose names to represent the moving data and what is known about the data.

TABLE 14.1  **Data Flow Charting Symbols**

| Name | Symbol | Definition |
|---|---|---|
| Data flow (represented by arrows) | REPORT-A | Arrows show the direction of the flow of data |
| Process (represented by rounded rectangles) | Identifier process name | A set of operations that transform data |
| Data store (represented by rectangles) | Data store name | Any place in a system where data is stored |
| External entity (represented by squares) | External entity | Sources and destinations of data outside of the system being designed |

## Second-Level Data Flow Diagram

The second-level diagram explodes the first level showing significant processes, data stores, and data flows in addition to the external entities. The objective of the second-level diagram is to show the following:

- The boundary of the system

- The major data stores

- The processes that maintain them

- The significant transactions representing recurring business events and the processes that analyze them

- The data stores used in those analyses

- The outputs that represent the results of immediate

- Transaction analysis

- The processes that summarize the business activity over a longer period.

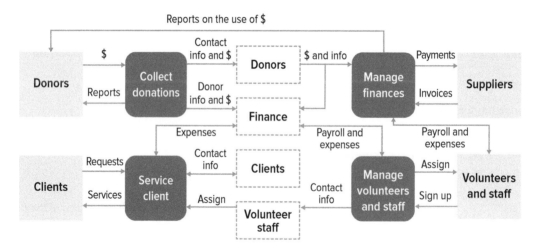

FIGURE 14.2  Second-level DFD shows four major processes and four major data stores

## Third-Level Data Flow Diagram

The objective of the lower-level diagram is to investigate more closely the subdivision of any upper-level processes. Each such diagram has a process name from the level above. Inputs and outputs related to external entities or data stores, as shown on the upper level, should appear at the boundary of the lower-level diagram. Less important data flows (such as control reports, error reports and corrections, etc.) should be added. Inside the boundary, the process should be exploded into components to show the different data transformations.

The lower level (third/fourth) diagram explodes the second level, showing process details. The data stores and external entities are the same as in the second level with more detailed flows.

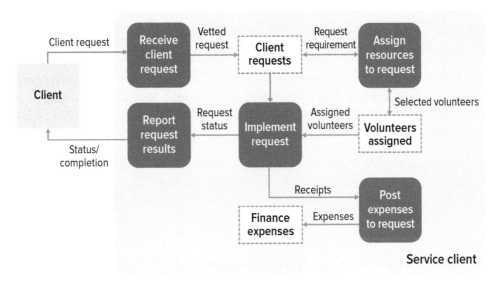

FIGURE 14.3  Third-level DFD of Service Client process

## 14.4 Guidelines for Constructing Data Flows

The following items summarize the steps involved in drawing up a data flow diagram for an existing or proposed system:

1. Identify the external entities involved. This involves deciding on a preliminary system boundary. If in doubt, include the first "outer layer" of manual and automated systems within the system boundary with which an interface is necessary. Remember that data flows are created when something happens in the outside world; a person decides to buy something, an accident happens, or a truck arrives at the loading bay. If possible, get back to the ultimate data source and draw the flow from there.

2. Identify the inputs and the outputs that can be expected and scheduled in the ordinary course of business. As the list grows, try to discover logical inputs and outputs groupings. Mark the inputs and outputs related solely to error and exception conditions.

3. Identify the inquiries and on-demand requests for information that could arise involving pairs of data flows, in which one data flow specifies what is "given" to the system. The second specifies what is "required" from the system.

4. Take a large sheet of paper and start on the left-hand side with the external entity that seems to be the prime source of inputs (e.g., customers). Draw the data flows that arise, logically necessary processes, and the data stores that seem to be required. Pay no attention to timing considerations except for natural, logical precedence and logically necessary data stores. Draw a system that never started and will never stop. It's sometimes helpful to follow a typical good input transaction through the system.

5.  Draw the first draft freehand, and concentrate on getting everything down, except errors, exceptions, and decisions. Decisions are made within low-level processes and do not appear on data flow diagrams.

6.  Accept that there will be a need for at least three drafts of the high-level data flow. Do not be concerned that the first draft looks like a hopeless tangle. It can be sorted out.

7.  When the first draft is completed, check the list of inputs and outputs to ensure that everything has been included except those that deal with errors and exceptions. Note any normal inputs and outputs that would not fit in on the draft. Remember that every data store that describes something in the real world must be created and maintained.

8.  Now produce a more precise second draft using a template for the symbols. Aim for a diagram with unique processes and the minimum number of crossing data flows. To minimize crossing,

    ▪ first, duplicate external entities if necessary

    ▪ next, duplicate data stores if necessary

    ▪ then allow data flows to cross if there is not a layout that reduces crossings.

    The second draft will look much more precise but will still have some unnecessary crossings, and the layout and relationship of process symbols could be improved. Check the list of inputs and outputs, and note anything that still cannot fit in on the second draft.

9.  Conduct a walkthrough of the second draft with the user representative, explaining that it is only a draft. Note any change resulting from the walkthrough.

10. Produce a lower-level explosion of each process defined on the second draft. Work out handling errors and exceptions and incorporate changes in the top-level diagram, if necessary. Then, the third and final version of the top-level diagram can be completed.

## 14.5 Multiple-Criteria Decision Analysis

Multiple-Criteria Decision Analysis (MCDA) is a decision-making analysis that evaluates multiple (conflicting) criteria as part of the decision-making process. Practically everyone in their daily lives uses this tool. Of course, humans make thousands of daily decisions, but this same process also occurs in the corporate world, government organizations, and medical centers.

MCDA resembles a cost-benefit analysis but with the notable advantage of not being solely limited to monetary units for its comparisons. When making comprehensive or important decisions, multiple criteria and scale levels must be accounted for. Comparing conflicting sets of criteria, such as quality and costs, can sometimes lead to confusion and lack of clarity. Making decisions based on multiple criteria with help from the MCDA tool can make things clear. By structuring complex problems and analyzing multiple sets of criteria, informed, more justifiable decisions can be made.

## Define the Context

Before you can start a multiple-criteria analysis, you need to define the context of your analysis clearly. The context accounts for the present situation, key players, and stakeholders in the decision-making process. Advantages of a clearly defined context are:

- Optimal allocation of resources toward accomplishing the objectives

- Improved communication between the different parties involved

- Facilitates multiple options

## Decide the Objectives and Select the Proper Criteria That Represent the Value

When buying a new car, the future owner wants to minimize potential costs and maximize the number of advantages. Prices are easy to compare, but advantages can be subject to varying interpretations. This is why these two goals conflict and can't be compared directly. In such cases, the advantages, where possible, need to be subdivided into quantifiable criteria, such as safety (crash-test result), comfort, luxury, reliability, and performance. As such, making decisions in a Multiple-Criteria Decision Analysis (MCDA) frequently comes down to matters of judgment. Purely objective assessments aren't always possible. But we can provide structure and make it easy for multiple decision-makers to participate and reach a consensus.

## Determine the Relative Importance of Each Criterion

The relative importance of something is what the car buyer notices when he or she has to choose between cars. The buyer can partially base their decision on the car's costs. But when they have made a short list of five cars they'd like to have, each differing $150 in price, that criterion suddenly loses importance. In contrast, a difference of $3,000 per car could have made this a weightier criterion for the buyer.

Therefore, the weighting of different criteria shows the difference between options and how relevant this difference is. For example, safety might weigh less heavily on the buyer's mind than maintenance costs because he or she considers it less important.

## Calculate the Different Values of the Criterion by Using Paired Comparisons

Paired **comparison** analysis helps you determine the importance of several options relative to one another. This makes it easy to choose the most important problem to solve or to pick the solution that will be most effective.

## Multiple-Criteria Decision Analysis (MCDA) Advantages

The use of a multiple-criteria analysis comes with various advantages when compared to a decision-making tool not based on specific criteria:

- The chosen criteria can be adjusted.

- Many different actors can be compared with one another.

- MCDA grants insight into different judgments of value.

- Scores and weights can be used as reference.

- It's an important means of communication between the different parties involved in the decision-making process.

## MCDA Example 1

Once the evaluation criteria are identified, the method's first step uses the three comparison codes and the corresponding symbol to compare each criterion and value. Table 14.2 below shows this using two criteria (1 and 2).

TABLE 14. 2  **\* Comparing 1 to 2**

| Importance | Symbol | Value* |
|---|---|---|
| Equally Important | = | 1,2 |
| More Important | > | 1 |
| Much More Important | >> | 1,1 |

The relative weight is determined using the paired comparison matrix methodology for each criterion. Then, the criteria are compared against each other and arranged in a matrix like below in Table 14.3.

TABLE 14.3  **MCDA Comparison Set-up**

| Criteria | 1 | 2 | 3 | 4 | Total | Relative Weight |
|---|---|---|---|---|---|---|
| 1 | 1 | | | | | |
| 2 | | 2 | | | | |
| 3 | | | 3 | | | |
| 4 | | | | 4 | | |
| | | | | | Total | 100% |

## MCDA Example 2

Criterion 1 is compared to criterion 2 and its importance is:

- Equal (=) shown as 1,2; or

- Greater than (>) shown as 1,1; or

- Much greater than (>>) shown as 1,1,1

Criterion 1 score is determined by adding the number of 1s in the row and column label 1. In the example below, that equals 6. To determine the score for criterion 2, add all the 2s in row 2 plus the 2s in column 2 above the 2 row, giving a score of 6. Each criterion total is determined likewise. Sum all the scores, giving a total score of 18 in the example below. The relative weight for each criterion is determined by dividing the criterion score by the total (18, Table 14.4). Show the relative weight as a percent.

TABLE 14.4  **MCDA Comparison Example**

| Criteria | 1 | 2 | 3 | 4 | Score | Relative Weight |
|---|---|---|---|---|---|---|
| 1 | 1 | 1,2 | 1,3 | 1,1,1 | 6 | 33% |
| 2 | | 2 | 2,2,2 | 2,4 | 6 | 33% |
| 3 | | | 3 | 3,3 | 4 | 22% |
| 4 | | | | 4 | 2 | 9% |
| | | | | Total | 18 | 100% |

## MCDA Total Weighted Score Example

Once the relative criterion weights are determined using the paired comparison matrix methodology, we can use the total weighted score to select a vendor, product, or service (VPS).

Arrange the vendors/products/services (VPS) and criteria as shown in the matrix below (Table 14.5). Score each VPS by assigning a point from 1 to 10:

- 0: Nonusable/functional;

- 3: Partially accomplished;

- 7: Mostly accomplished; and

- 10: Fully accomplished.

Multiply the points by the weight, giving the score for each criterion. Sum the scores to obtain the overall total score for the VPS. The highest total score is the VPS that should be selected unless other factors affect the selections.

TABLE 14.5 **VPS Total Score**

| | | Vendor A | | | Vendor B | |
|---|---|---|---|---|---|---|
| Criteria | Points | Weight | Score | Points | Weight | Score |
| | | | | | | |
| | | | | | | |
| | | | | | | |
| | | | | | | |
| | | | | | | |
| VPS TOTAL Score: | | 100% | | | 100% | |

## 14.6 The Minto Principle

You as a consultant must structure your thinking. This is the best way to present your ideas clearly to clients. One excellent tool is the pyramid principle, conceived by ex-McKinsey consultant Barbara Minto (Minto, 1987). She authored *The Minto Pyramid Principle*, which essentially defined the way consultants structure most of their presentations. Most consultants will know the pyramid principle, even if they don't know the author.

Consultants often use groupings to clarify and simplify problems. Unfortunately, consultants are skeptical enough to believe that many business problems are similar. Too often, clients are entrenched in their industry, corporate culture, and personal experience to rise above and see the root causes or drivers. The typical client critique of a consultants is, "Well, of course, I could have told you that." The (unspoken) consulting rebuttal might be, "Yes, but you did not have the clarity of thought and persuasion to get your point across."

The **Pyramid Principle** advocates that "ideas should always form a pyramid under a single thought." The single thought is the answer to the key question. Underneath the single thought, you should group and summarize the next level of supporting ideas and arguments. People ideally work out their thinking by creating pyramids of ideas:

- Grouping together low-level facts they see as similar;

- Drawing insight from having seen the similarity;

- Forming a new group of related insights, etc.

The first step in a consulting assignment using the Minto principle is to define the client's problem statement (see Figure 14.4). We can do this via the SCQ method:

- Understand the situation;

- Determine the complication;

- Formulate the key question.

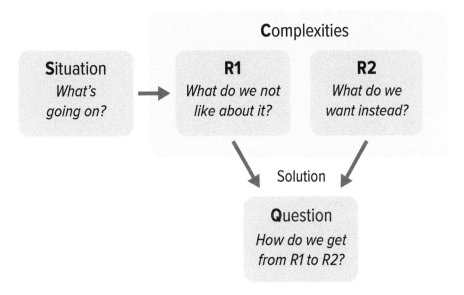

FIGURE 14.4  SQC diagram (Minto, 1987)

We determine the key answer from the problem statement question (See Figure 14.5). The key answer needs to be crisp, actionable, and unambiguous. We add to the pyramid by building upon issues and sub-issues until we reach the root cause.

1. Put the key statement answering your key question at the top of the pyramid.

2. Drill down the key statement into the relevant issues.

3. Differentiate between issues and sub-issues and sort them logically (MECE—see Section below).

4. Follow each path to identify the root causes.

5. Check whether all requirements of a pyramid are fulfilled and meet the main rules of a pyramid. It should answer the key question and be built in a logical vertical order; ideas at any level in the pyramid must always be summaries of the ideas grouped below them, and ideas in each grouping must always be the same kind of idea

There are three parts to the pyramid formed from the facts, questions, and insights:

- Answer: Incite level 1: recommendation for actions (top of the pyramid)

- Second layer: Arguments that support your answer (3 to 5 arguments) incite level 2

- Bottom: Data that supports your arguments

The pyramid style starts with answering a key question (problem statement) and engages through clear, explicit logic and persuasion to support decision-making in a business context.

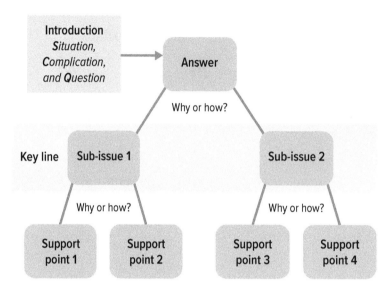

FIGURE 14.5   Minto pyramid (Minto, 1987)

## The MECE Principle

The **MECE** (Minto, 1987) framework segments a set into subsets exclusively and exhaustively. **MECE** is an acronym that stands for mutually exclusive (**ME**) and collectively exhaustive (**CE**). When a categorization (sub-setting) is both mutually exclusive and collectively exhaustive, we can say that it is **MECE** (**MECE** is pronounced *me-see*).

- Mutually exclusive: There is no overlap among subsets.

- Collectively exhaustive: Every element of the set is included in a subset.

We can trace similar logical methods back thousands of years to Aristotle and similar ancient thinkers. The MECE concept in the consulting world was invented by Barbara Minto of McKinsey and popularized in her book *The Pyramid Principle*.

### A Simple MECE Example of Classifying Cars
Let's classify cars into two groups: red cars and sports cars.

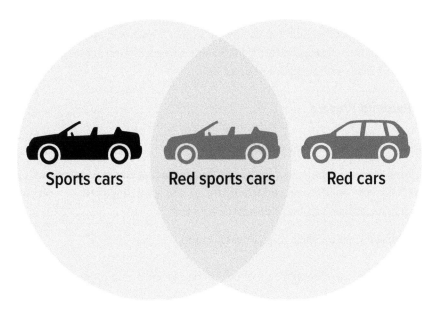

FIGURE 14.6  MECE example 1

This classification is clearly not MECE. A car can be both red and a sports car. This classification thus fails on a simple test of mutual exclusivity (ME). The intersection between our two sets of red cars and sports cars would have to be empty to be mutually exclusive. That would require the world to contain no red sports cars.

This classification is also not collectively exhaustive (CE) because a blue hatchback is outside both categories.

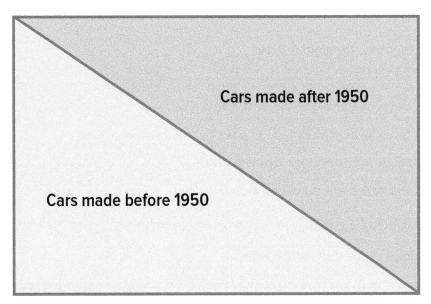

FIGURE 14.7  MECE example 2

A classification that's MECE would be to divide cars into those made up to and after 1950. The same car could not have been made before and after 1950, so this categorization is Mutually Exclusive. It is also Exhaustive, as any car is made either before or after 1950.

### Summary of the Pyramid Process

- The key statement at the top of your pyramid answers the key question.

- The issues and sub-issues are built in a logical order supporting the key statement. For example, is the question "why" or "how" answered when you go one level down? (If so, you can stop drilling down.) Or do your sub-issues call for additional evidence?

- The sub-issues are separate on each layer/in each group.

  - Mutually exclusive: no overlapping sub-issues on one layer/in one group.

  - Collectively exhaustive: sub-issues are comprehensive.

- There should be the lowest possible number of sub-issues on each layer/in each group—the fewer, the better. If you have more than five sub-issues, consider whether you really should have another, separate issue branch above.

- The sub-issues on one layer/in one group are structured in a logical order. Inductive reasoning is mainly used to structure thoughts. Deductive reasoning is mainly used to structure communication to audiences that need to be convinced

### Rules to Check That Your Pyramid Is Good

There are three pyramid rules:

- Ideas at any level must summarize the ideas grouped below them.

- Ideas in each grouping must be part of the same logical argument in each.

- The argument must be in strict logical order—MECE.

- The pyramid structure forces a question/answer dialogue.

  - The main point raises a question. (For example, How? Why?)

  - You answer the question on the line below.

  - You continue to raise and answer questions until it is clear why you say what you say.

  There are two kinds of logical answers, deductive and inductive:

- Deductive: The second point comments on the first, third point states the implication of the first two.

- Inductive: Ideas are all of the same kind (same subject or same predicate), ideas can be described by a plural noun (e.g., steps, reasons).

There are three kinds of inductive order:

- Time: If you got the ideas by working out cause-and-effect relationships

- Degree: If you got the ideas by classifying

- Structural: If you got the ideas by visualizing an analytical framework

Check to reveal problems in the order of a grouping:

- Distinguish causes from their effect.

- Question the assumption behind the point.

- Isolate the keyword in each point.

- Make the "I" test on actions.

- Use deductive reasoning only if the argument is more important than the action:

  - Because the reader expects a different answer from yours, or

  - Because they cannot understand the action without prior explanation.

- An "issue" is a question phrased as to demand a "yes" or "no" answer.

## 14.7 Successful Meetings

Running meetings is a key and most frequent activity of consulting. A meeting aims to discuss and exchange one or more ideas. Although discussing ideas face-to-face is the one activity that can't be done anywhere else, Zoom (or similar product) meetings are the only reasonable alternatives. This interaction and exchange of ideas, whether to reach a decision or resolve a dispute, is the unique function of a meeting.

A potential pitfall is to call a meeting when the purpose is to deliver a presentation. Sometimes, a brief presentation during a meeting is helpful, but presenting ideas can be done more effectively in other settings. In addition, meeting presentations may break the interactive tone needed to exchange ideas.

The following approach to managing meetings emphasizes understanding and working with the three components of effective meetings: content, structure, and process. The goal is to increase the probability that you will conduct an effective meeting. Within these components, this section includes:

- Pre-meeting planning and preparation;

- Guidelines for conducting a meeting;

- Keeping the meeting on track;

- Obtaining relevant information;

- Overcoming objections and resistance;

- Achieving the meeting's goal; and

- Follow-up to ensure meeting outcomes are carried out.

IMAGE 14.1

## Preparation for Holding a Meeting

Several steps must be performed to prepare for a successful meeting properly.

1. Define the goal. What do you want to accomplish?

2. Determine the type of meeting to achieve the goal.

3. Select the time and place.

4. Select and order agenda items.

5. Select and contact attendees. Whether leading or setting up a meeting, think about the power structure. For example, who should be in attendance to help you achieve the objective, given the goal?

6. Send agenda to attendees before the meeting; confirm attendance.

7. Shape a participative room/seating environment.

8. Research the group:

   - What is the power structure of the invitees?

   - What resources are available in the group to help you achieve the goal? What resources do you need that may not be there? How can you adapt or get the resources?

   - What is the structure? Who will be at the meeting? Try to distinguish between overt power ("I'm the boss, and you report to me") and informal power, such as the person with more influence than their position might indicate.

   - What will be the likely resistance, and from whom? How will you handle it?

- Are certain people often disruptive? Anticipate how to handle them.

- In meetings with a client, the objective may be to get another contract or focus on who will do what and when. You may not know who will attend the meeting. You can, however, gain data. Before the meeting, ask positively, "Can you tell me about it so I can best prepare?" Ask straightforward questions about each person's function and their relationship with others.

- With in-house meetings, the parameters are different, and you can be more at ease. You still need to know the people in order to develop working relationships.

Developing a goal focuses a meeting leader and participants on what needs to be accomplished. It also helps to plan a meeting's content, process, and structure.

Develop the goal with a specific statement on the outcomes to be achieved. Sample outcome statements might be to:

- Build the working relationship of a team.

- Enhance the working relationship between the two departments.

- Improve the response time of our sale lead generation program.

- Respond to a competitor's new advertising campaign.

- Improve how our clients relate to their customers.

These desired outcomes determine the content of an agenda. Next, select the process to achieve the outcomes. What process may work best?

- Exchange of information.

- Brainstorming session.

- Analytical problem solving.

- Evaluation and discussion.

- A mixture of any or all of the above.

Finally, determine the structure. How will decisions about outcomes be reached? Will it be parliamentary (consensus, vote) or cabinet-style decisions reached by the chairperson? There are two structural styles:

- Parliamentary-style meeting: the leader is more a facilitator, less a director. A vote count or consensus determines what will happen.

- Cabinet-style meeting: the leader makes their decision after hearing participants' advice.

It is best if groups and leaders are clear about the structure. Both structures are legitimate modes if attendees understand them and the power structure.

## Guidelines for Conducting the Meeting

1. Keep your tone conversational, personal, open, and direct.

2. Listen for intent, not just the words or tone. Speak to the intent.

3. When a question is asked, look at the questioner, and interrupt only to clarify.

4. Give your answer to the group if you want to avoid dialogue.

5. If the room's acoustics are poor, repeat the question.

6. If you lack the answer, say so, and indicate how and when you will respond.

7. Try to remain calm in the face of an antagonistic, hostile question.

8. Rephrase hostile questions with positive words to remove the sting.

   - Question: "Isn't your company truly cheating customers with these cheap plastic inserts?"

   - Response: "Regarding the quality of our products ..."

9. When a question refers to a topic beyond your knowledge, defer to another person or indicate when and how you will get back to the questioner:

   "I am not the best person to answer that. Let me have So-and-So, who works directly on that line, get back to you. Give me your telephone number, and I will make sure he calls you as soon as possible."

10. Knowing when to bring an item to closure is a matter of timing about when to complete the discussion of an item, or if its importance requires postponing other, less essential items. The guidelines include the following:

    a. To determine if people are ready to reach closure, listen to each person's tone. For example, are people animated and expectant to get closure, or are they quiet and detached?

    b. Are questions about specific problems or issues in the abstract? Are questions asking for more detail, or are they general without purpose?

    c. Are people sitting turned toward you or away from you?

    d. Do people look at you or away from you?

    e. Answers to these questions help gauge when to continue or end the discussion.

    Before asking for closure:

    - Try to ensure that everyone has an adequate opportunity to express their views.

    - Acknowledge each person's views.

    - Take a vote or indicate you have all the information that is needed.

If you feel it is time to move on to the next item, ask for a wrap-up of the discussion. You might ask: "Does anyone have any final words?"

After gaining closure, wrap up the meeting.

- ▪ Summarize key meeting outcomes.

- ▪ Review next steps and assignments given.

- ▪ If needed, set a "next meeting" date.

- ▪ Indicate when minutes/post-meeting reports will be distributed.

- ▪ Ask for an evaluation of the meeting.

- ▪ Thank people for their contributions.

## Successful Meeting Checklist

Preparation:

- Determine if a meeting is required. Define the purpose. Does the cost justify it? If not, consider alternatives.

- Develop an agenda based on your goal.

- Choose attendees based on the goal.

- Learn about attendees; what are the overt and covert power structures?

- Anticipate likely resistance; how will you encounter it?

- Choose a process: brainstorm, information exchange, problem-solve, other.

- Determine the decision-making process.

- Choose the time, place, furniture arrangements, and refreshments.

- Send the agenda to attendees in advance and confirm attendance.

- Make provisions for someone to take notes and minutes.

Conducting the meeting:

- Arrive early to ensure the room is prepared so you can start on time.

- Introduce yourself to attendees when they arrive.

- Start by outlining the goal, expected outcomes, and the agenda.

- Review the process for reaching decisions.

- Gain agreement on how interruptions will be handled.

- Review previous meeting reports and follow-up actions.

- Keep the meeting moving to get closure on each agenda item.

- Take the pulse: be sensitive to verbal and nonverbal cues.

- Gain closure on each item: next steps, assignments, and follow-up.

End of the meeting:

- Summarize outcomes and processes to ensure people do what they said they would do.

- If needed, select the next meeting date and time.

- Indicate when post-meeting reports will be issued.

- Thank people for their contribution.

Follow-up:

- Prepare and send post-meeting reports/minutes to attendees.

- Conduct any necessary follow-up.

## Checklist for Being Influential at In-person Meetings

**Empathetic listening** is the key to being influential. It's not enough to be smart and well researched and correct, even (especially) when you have the evidence to prove it. You have to earn the right to be valid. Others will listen to you and be open to your advice and point of view once they feel you have fully heard and understood them. They have to "get that you get them." Seek to understand, and you will be understood.

**Influencing by listening** is not easy for most people. Business people in particular are trained to think in linear terms, believe in persuasion by PowerPoint, and count on the power of logic. "To influence, you must listen" may sound like, "To do something, don't do anything." You must redirect your can-do, get-results attitude to one of subtle influence by sitting back and listening.

Here is a five-point checklist for being more influential in meetings:

1. Before you enter the meeting, take one minute to prepare your mind:

   - Quietly detach from the outcome. Accept that the participants may not accept your advice. Loosen your grip on the results. You have done all the prep work. As good golfers say, "Trust your swing."

   - Remind yourself that the objective of the meeting is to reach a decision or resolve a dispute. In addition, to improve relationships with the other participants.

■ Be willing to be influenced in the process. Be open to ideas, collaboration, and the learning that results. Allow yourself to be confidently vulnerable.

2. When you state your point of view during a meeting, say it crisply and simply. Do not take much time. Do not overstate. Keep it simple and to the point.

3. Spend the majority of your time listening. Cultivate an attitude of curiosity about what is being said and what is coming next. You will know you have listened well when others naturally turn the conversation back to you ("Joe, what do you think?").

4. When you get the cue that it is your turn to be listened to, be sure to build on what has been said. Lead with what you liked about what you heard, make linkages, and expand ideas. If you have concerns, express them separately and with curiosity. "Would you share with me your thoughts on that?"

5. When the conversation begins to conclude, summarize the outcome. If you are dissatisfied, go back to point 2: state your point of view and listen more.

## Checklist for Being Influential in Remote, Online, Zoom Meetings

1. **Position yourself properly:** Projecting executive presence starts by taking up space, literally and figuratively. Sitting too far away from the camera makes you appear small, which can subconsciously signal that you're less powerful, nervous, or otherwise disengaged. Fix this by positioning your camera to show the area from your upper chest to your head. Make sure the top of your head isn't chopped off and that there are a few inches of visual space above your crown.

2. **Look level:** You garner the most trust by establishing strong eye contact with your audience. Therefore, keep your camera at eye level. Do this by propping your laptop or webcam on a stack of books.

3. **Light it up:** Avoid sitting with your back to a window or being backlit by a lamp. When possible, take video calls with a window in front of you.

4. **Smile at the camera, not your colleagues:** Practice looking straight into the camera rather than glancing at your image on the screen. Placing a sticky note with a smiley face right above your webcam will help.

5. **Say no to virtual backgrounds:** Virtual backgrounds are problematic. Instead, use a neutral and professional backdrop, such as an office space with shelves in view. Don't shy away from personal elements like photos of the family. These are great conversation starters that humanize you and build connections.

6. **Use a strong voice:** Use a good-quality headset. In this digital age, your audio quality is part of the overall picture of your presence. Speak slightly faster than you would in person to hold people's attention.

7. **Stay stable:** Do not slouch or hunch over during video calls. Instead, send signals of competency and warmth by relaxing your shoulders and pulling them down your back. Looking at ease creates a positive perception in the eyes of the people you're trying to influence.

8. **Know about notifications:** Mute your desktop notifications before a call. All the dings and pings are disrespectful to the people on the call. Instead, make others feel important by demonstrating they have your full attention. Also, be aware that anything you say in the chat will be visible in the final transcript—something you'd be comfortable with your boss seeing.

9. **Get your mindset right:** Executive presence is more than your visual look and body language. Fundamentally, it's about your mentality. And nothing detracts from projecting an air of confidence like undermining yourself.

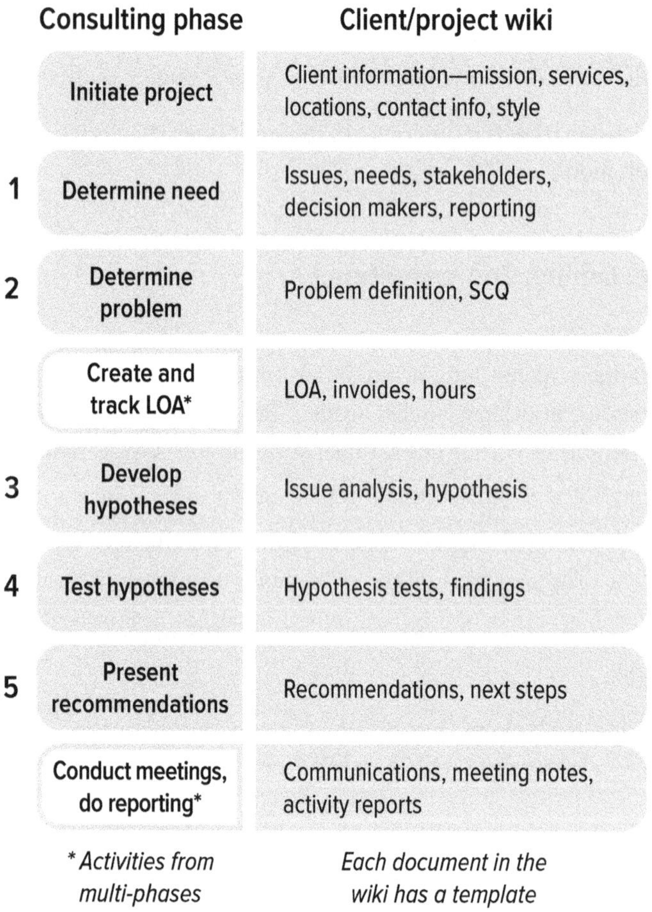

| Consulting phase | Client/project wiki |
|---|---|
| Initiate project | Client information—mission, services, locations, contact info, style |
| 1 Determine need | Issues, needs, stakeholders, decision makers, reporting |
| 2 Determine problem | Problem definition, SCQ |
| Create and track LOA* | LOA, invoides, hours |
| 3 Develop hypotheses | Issue analysis, hypothesis |
| 4 Test hypotheses | Hypothesis tests, findings |
| 5 Present recommendations | Recommendations, next steps |
| Conduct meetings, do reporting* | Communications, meeting notes, activity reports |

*Activities from multi-phases*          *Each document in the wiki has a template*

FIGURE 14.8  Wiki project documentation

## 14.8 Documenting a Consulting Engagement

A consulting engagement (project) should maintain documentation throughout the project, from authorization until final sign-off. Then it should be archived as a reference for further assignments. The best way is to set up a client/engagement wiki. Many software products (use one that is Cloud based) exist to create and maintain the wiki.

A simple structure and content should be maintained in the wiki, as shown in the following figure. The design and content are based on this book's chapters on conducting a consulting project.

Therefore, the documentation in the repository should be organized first by the client and then by engagement (project). Documentation collected during the engagement is collected by stage of the engagement. See the sample organization in Figure 14.8.

## 14.9 HT Fitness Case

Harry Smith and Tom Jones founded HT Fitness in the 1980s. Gyms and workout facilities grew in the 1970s and continued into the 1980s, especially in the metropolitan areas. The 1980s brought cheap strip mall properties with the overbuilding and savings and loan failures. Harry and Tom both had promising careers and saw the opportunity to start what they hoped would be a growing industry and business. They grew the company to ten locations around the city.

Harry worked as a vice president of a savings and loan bank, which went bankrupt in the 1980s during the downfall of all the savings and loan banks. Harry was a very entrepreneurial guy who always had a vision of making money and was image conscious about everything like driving a BMW or being the first guy with an Apple watch—all the trimmings of financial success. So, with time on his hands, he decided to look at options for himself besides banking.

Harry loved the whole idea of entrepreneurs and starting companies. He looked for other opportunities and noticed that there was lots of space available in strip centers because of the cheap properties at the S&Ls. He loved working out at gyms and had done it his entire life. He had excellent ideas about what a top gym should look like and what facilities it should provide.

Harry asked his good friend Tom Jones, a college friend, about a fitness center opportunity and what he thought about it. Tom is a friendly guy who never met a stranger and who had worked his way up to director of sales for an athletic supply company.

Harry convinced him they should look into the fitness center business, emphasizing weight training because that's what they had done together since college. In addition, they had worked out together at several different gyms over the years.

Harry and Tom began investigating available properties and working on a business plan. First, they calculated how much startup money they would need, how many and what kind of staff they would need, ideas on marketing the center, and projected cash flow and profit. Next, they visited the Service Corps of Retired Executives (SCORE) to discuss their business plan and finance ideas.

SCORE—"Counselors to America's Small Business"—is a nonprofit association comprised of 13,000+ volunteer business counselors throughout the United States and its territories. SCORE members are trained to serve as counselors, advisers, and mentors to aspiring entrepreneurs and business owners.

SCORE reviewed and edited Harry and Tom's business plan, resulting in a Small Business Administration loan. As a result, they began their new business with the name of HT (as in Harry/Tom) Fitness Center. Their business boomed from the beginning.

HT Fitness Center began opening new centers and decided they needed help managing their finances. Tom had become terrific friends with George Chan and helped him with his workout routines. George was a lead accountant at a retail chain. He was a very focused, clean-desk kind of guy. George often worked out at one of the HT Fitness Centers. Tom and Harry explained to George their expansion plans and needed somebody with a financial background. After some discussions, they talked George into joining them to help expand the HT Fitness Centers.

After decades of steady growth in their business, the membership started declining at an alarming rate. Over the past five years, the total membership number had decreased an average of 6% annually. Each of the executives (Harry, Tom, and George) had a different idea of why this was happening. So, after much discussion and monthly reviews of the declining membership numbers, they hired a consultant to determine what was causing the decline and make recommendations on how to reverse the trend and start growing again.

They discussed their situation with a consultant they had used before when they were starting up. The consultant helped the executives to define their problems.

## Problem Statement

Example: How to increase membership?

Two issues were defined to help answer the problem definition question:

1. Why is HT Fitness Centers' membership declining?

2. How to get and retain new members?

## Information Collected by the Consultant

The consultant thought this case's focus should be on the market segmentation and determining/targeting the optimal segment. The consultant understood that profit is the ultimate goal.

Various strategies will have different implementation costs and potential revenues. The consultant returned to the profitability numbers at every step of the analysis. The consultant put together some relevant data gathered through interviews and research.

Relevant data:

- Gym memberships in this city have been growing 3% each year, both in this city and in all regions of the country.

- HT Fitness gyms offer cardio rooms, free weights, and weight machines.

- Membership prices and payment plans are in line with their closest competitors.

- HT Fitness targets serious fitness enthusiasts, believing that these are the most loyal customers.

- HT Fitness uses the local press for its marketing campaigns.

Analysis of data and identification of potential causes:

- Changing fitness trends, such as class-based fitness or high-intensity training

- Negative attributes of HT Fitness, such as poor customer service or locations in deteriorating neighborhoods

- Competitors offer better services, such as personal trainers or basketball courts

- Shifts in the city or industry demographics away from HT Fitness Centers' target demographic area

- Not reaching the desired clients with targeted information

Analysis of data and identification of unlikely causes:

- Decreasing city population (as the rest of the city's gyms see increasing memberships)

- Competitors offer lower fees (already established that HTF's fees are comparable to competitors)

Findings from interviews with HTF executives, center managers, and research:

- Local gym memberships are trending toward the 30–40 age group and 40–50 age group and away from the 18–30 age groups, baby boomers, and seniors based on their market of serious fitness enthusiasts

- Gender seems to have shifted toward men, then back to women

- HTF membership is heavily concentrated in the 18–30 age group

- HTF membership is evenly split between men and women

- HTF's membership gender profile parallels the local industry gender profile

- HTF's membership generation profile is focused on the declining millennial population rather than the growing Gen X and Y populations

Conclusions from the interviews:

- Need to target Gen X and Y customers or

- Become more of a niche gym for the declining millennial customer segment

Review of conclusions and findings with HTF leadership:

- After reviewing this data, HTF leadership agreed that they should target Gen X and Y customers but are unwilling to give up the 18–30 age group because they are the bulk of their membership. The consultant then investigated:

  - What are some possible ways that HT Fitness can target these identified demographics?

  - What would be the risks/rationale of each of these recommendations?

## Brainstorm Possible Recommendations by the Consultant

Consultant brainstorm of possible recommendations:

- Marketing campaign targeting consumers aged 30–50

  - Spokesperson in that age range

  - Ads run in areas of interest for these consumers

  - Use of digital media rather than print

  - An explanation that this gym is for these consumers (à la Planet Fitness ads)

- Offer new services more to the liking of middle-aged customers, but do not lose the other base

- Make prices more appealing to middle-aged customers. If the price is believed to be a primary concern, lower prices. If not, raising prices would help offer more services and prevent younger customers with less disposable income from joining

- Make the gym an exclusive club where only those members can join.

### Consultant's Issues Analysis

The consultant analyzed the issues, including developing hypotheses for each sub-issue to determine the causes of decline and potential options to grow the business. This would structure the analysis and help determine what detailed data may still be needed to answer the problem statement the consultant and the HTF executives had agreed on. In addition, the analysis of the issues would point to additional data required to test the hypotheses. Finally, testing the hypotheses would result in conclusions and their rationale as the basis for recommendations. The charts below show some of the consultant's data and information in performing the issue analysis and testing the hypotheses.

Issues analysis, hypotheses development, data gathering, and testing hypotheses, including developing recommendations, are left to the reader. What do you think the consultant recommended?

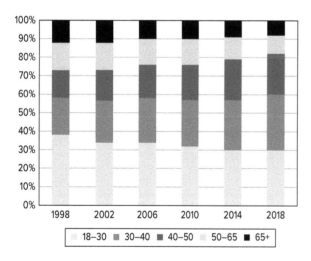

CHART 14.1  Age Distribution of Client Base for 20 Years

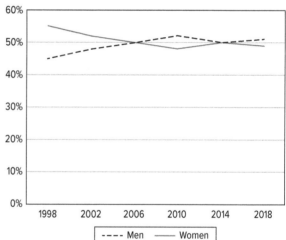

CHART 14.2  Gender Breakdown of Client Base

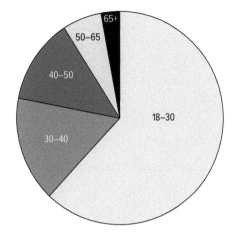

CHART 14.3  Client Customers by Generation

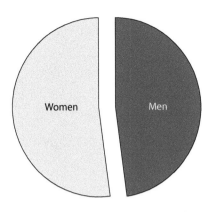

CHART 14.4  Client Customers by Gender

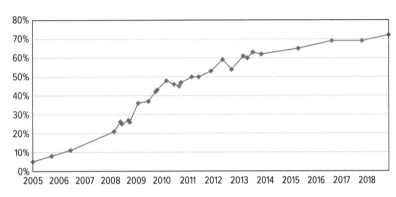

CHART 14.5  Social Media Use over Time

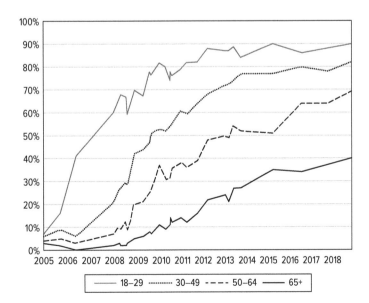

CHART 14.6  Who Uses Social Media? Percent of US Adults Who Use at Least
One Social Media Site, by Age

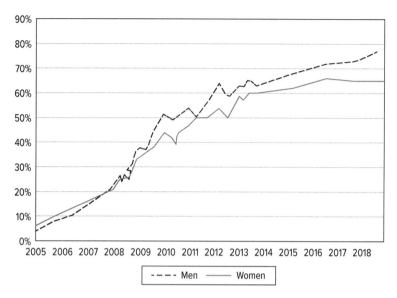

CHART 14.7  Percent of US Adults Who Use at Least One Social Media Site, by Gender

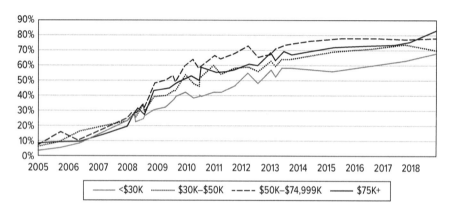

CHART 14.8  Percent of US Adults Who Use at Least One Social Media Site, by Income

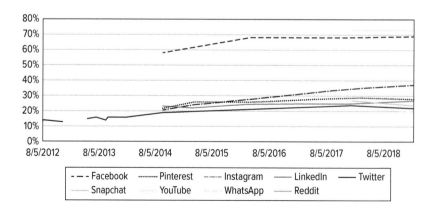

CHART 14.9  Which Social Media Platforms Are Most Popular?

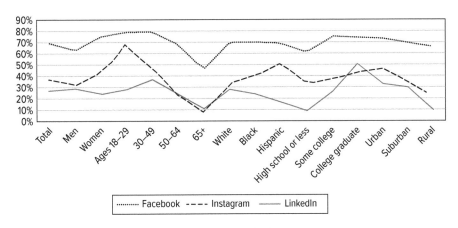

CHART 14.10   Who Uses Facebook, Instagram, or LinkedIn?

CHART 14.11   **Percent of US Adults in Each Age Group Who Say They Use**

|  | 50+ | 30–49 | 25–49 | 28–24 |
|---|---|---|---|---|
| YouTube | 56% | 90% | 90% | 94% |
| Facebook | 55% | 80% | 80% | 80% |
| Snapchat | 7% | 25% | 55% | 78% |
| Instagram | 16% | 40% | 55% | 71% |
| Twitter | 14% | 25% | 32% | 45% |

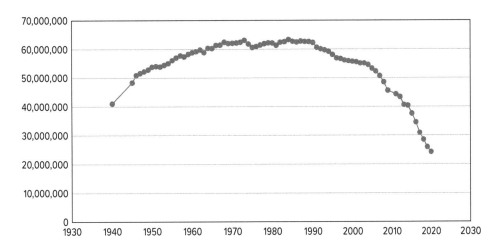

CHART 14.12   Daily Newspaper Readership From 1998 to 2018

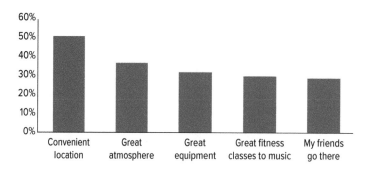

CHART 14.13  What Drives People into Fitness Facilities?

CHART 14.14  **Why Are They Exercising?**

|  | All Ages | Millennials |
|---|---|---|
| Get and maintain health | 40% | 27% |
| Maintain shape | 32% | 17% |
| Fun | 31% | 33% |
| Calming/relaxing | 23% | 16% |

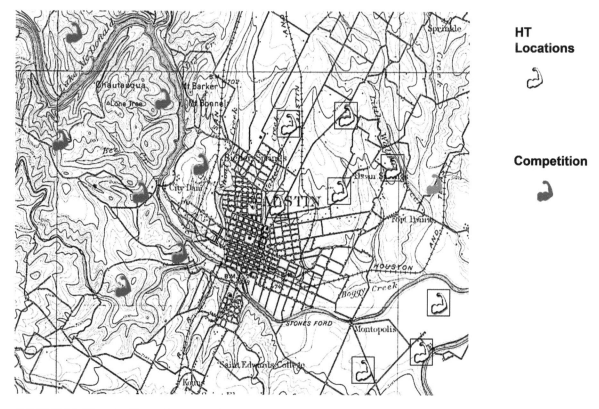

**HT
Locations**

**Competition**

CHART 14.15  Where Are Fitness Center Locations?

## Case Problem Summary

The problem statement: How to increase membership?

- Understand the situation

- Determine the complication

- Formulate the key question

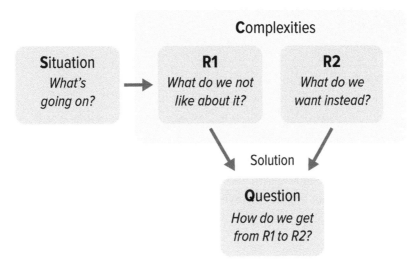

FIGURE 14.9  The problem statement (Minto, 1986)

Situation: Membership is declining

- R1: Losing Members

- R2: Increase Membership

Solution/Question: How to increase membership?

Main issues that need to be answered:

- What is the source of HT Fitness Centers' declining membership?

- What does HT Fitness need to do to mitigate the decline and increase membership?

### Data Resources

Great resource for social media statistics: https://www.pewresearch.org/internet/fact-sheet/social-media/
Great resource for demographics of all types: https://www.census.gov/quickfacts/fact/table/US/PST045221

## 14.10 Fishbone/Ishikawa Diagram

A fishbone diagram, also known as an Ishikawa diagram or a cause-and-effect diagram, is a visual tool used to identify the root causes of a problem. It is an effective method for analyzing business problems, as it allows you to break down the problem into its various causes and sub-causes. Examples of uses of the fishbone diagram include the following:

- To analyze a problem statement

- To brainstorm the causes of the problem (root cause analysis)

- To analyze a new design

- Process improvement

- Quality improvement

  The following steps show how to use a fishbone diagram to analyze a business problem.

### Identify the Problem

The first step in using a fishbone diagram is to clearly define the problem you want to analyze. This could be a business issue such as low sales, high employee turnover, or a lack of customer satisfaction.

### Draw the Diagram

Draw a horizontal line across the page and write the problem statement at the right end of the line. This is the "head" of the fish. Next, draw a diagonal line from the head towards the left, sloping downwards. This will form the "spine" of the fish. Finally, draw small horizontal lines perpendicular to the spine at the end of each diagonal line. These will be the "bones" of the fish.

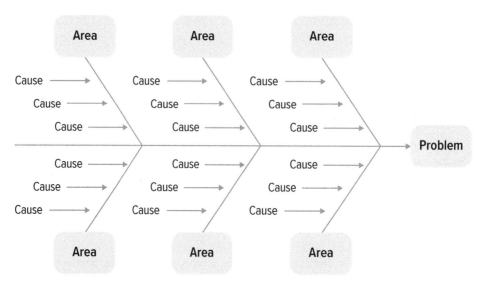

FIGURE 14.10  Fishbone diagram

## Identify the Categories

Label each bone with a category (like an Area as in figure 14.10) that might contribute to the problem. For example, if the problem is low sales, you might use categories such as marketing, pricing, product design, or customer service. The categories will depend on the nature of the problem you are analyzing

## Brainstorm the Causes

Next, brainstorm the possible causes of the problem and write them as sub-causes under each category. This is where you will identify the root causes of the problem. For example, if the problem is low sales, you might list under the marketing category sub-causes such as ineffective advertising, poor targeting, or lack of promotion.

## Analyze the Causes

Now that you have identified the potential causes, you can analyze each cause and its relationship to the problem. This will help you identify the most significant causes and prioritize your efforts. You can use various methods, such as data analysis or process mapping, to analyze the causes.

## Take Action

Once you have identified the root causes of the problem, you can develop and implement solutions to address them. By using a fishbone diagram to analyze the problem, you can be confident that you have thoroughly examined all possible causes and developed a comprehensive solution.

In conclusion, using a fishbone diagram is an effective method for analyzing business problems. By breaking down the problem into its various causes and sub-causes, you can identify the root causes and develop a comprehensive solution to address the problem. With practice, you can become skilled at using this tool to solve a wide range of business problems

### END NOTES

Steps in business consulting to complete a case assignment:

1. Find and acquire a client or potential client.

2. Determine the client's explicit needs.

3. Frame the explicit needs as an agreed problem statement.

4. Brainstorm issues that may have caused the problem.

5. Perform issue analysis.

6. Brainstorm hypotheses for each sub-issue.

7. Determine data needed (interviews, surveys, research) to test the hypotheses.

8. Perform tests on the hypotheses.

9. From the hypotheses' testing results, determine conclusions and findings.

10. From the conclusions and findings, develop recommendations.

11. Document the findings and recommendations in a consultant report and present it to the client.

## REFERENCES

Covey, Stephen R. *The 7 Habits of Highly Effective People.* Simon & Schuster, 2020.

Gane, Chris, and Trish Sarson. *Structured System Analysis: Tools and Techniques.* Improved System Technologies, 1977.

Heiser, Marshall. *DMCC Casebook: Heavy Things Fitness CASE 4, Duke Consulting Club,* p. 45, 2014–2015.

Minto, Barbara. *The Pyramid Principle: Logic in Writing and Thinking.* Minto International, 1986.

Pew Research Center. *Social Media Fact Sheet, 2022.* https://www.pewresearch.org/internet/fact-sheet/social-media/

Superior IS. *Successful Meetings.* Houston: Copyrighted Material, 2014.

Superior IS. *VMAP Methodology.* Houston: Copyrighted Material, 2014.

Superior IS. *Technology Selection Methodology.* Houston: Copyrighted Material, 2014.

# Index

Milton Keynes UK
Ingram Content Group UK Ltd.
UKHW050234010224
436936UK00032B/370

9 798823 330442